# U.S. Captive Insurance Law

# U.S. Captive Insurance Law

**F. Hale Stewart**
JD, LLM, CAM, CWM, CTEP

iUniverse, Inc.
Bloomington

# U.S. Captive Insurance Law

Copyright © 2010 by F. Hale Stewart, JD, LLM, CAM, CWM, CTEP

All rights reserved. No part of this book may be used or reproduced by any means, graphic, electronic, or mechanical, including photocopying, recording, taping or by any information storage retrieval system without the written permission of the publisher except in the case of brief quotations embodied in critical articles and reviews.

iUniverse books may be ordered through booksellers or by contacting:

iUniverse
1663 Liberty Drive
Bloomington, IN 47403
www.iuniverse.com
1-800-Authors (1-800-288-4677)

Because of the dynamic nature of the Internet, any Web addresses or links contained in this book may have changed since publication and may no longer be valid. The views expressed in this work are solely those of the author and do not necessarily reflect the views of the publisher, and the publisher hereby disclaims any responsibility for them.

Any people depicted in stock imagery provided by Thinkstock are models, and such images are being used for illustrative purposes only.

Certain stock imagery © Thinkstock.

ISBN: 978-1-4502-7794-5 (sc)
ISBN: 978-1-4502-7795-2 (ebk)

Printed in the United States of America

iUniverse rev. date: 01/03/2011

# Contents

**Introduction** ..................................... 1

Part I: Captive Insurance Basics......................... 3
  **Who Should Form a Captive?** ....................... 3
  **What Are the Benefits of a Captive Insurance Company?** .. 5
  **What Type of Captive Should a Company Form?** ..... 12
  **What Type of Corporate Structure Should I Use?** ..... 22
  **How to Form a Captive** .......................... 27
    Domicile Selection .............................. 27
    Feasibility Study................................ 31
  **Steps to Form a Captive in US Jurisdictions** .......... 36
  **Running the Captive** ............................ 39
  **Shutting Down the Captive** ...................... 44
  **Taxation** ...................................... 44
    Small Insurance Company Election under 831(b) ..... 60
    Foreign Captives................................ 62

Part II: A Case Law History of Captive Insurance ......... 69
  **Introduction** .................................. 69
    An Introduction to the History of US Captive Insurance
    Case Law ..................................... 69
    The Non-Deductibility of Reserves.................. 76

    Helvering . . . . . . . . . . . . . . . . . . . . . . . . . . . . . . . . . . 84
    Moline Properties . . . . . . . . . . . . . . . . . . . . . . . . . . . . . 87
    The Flood Plane Cases . . . . . . . . . . . . . . . . . . . . . . . . . . 89
    Consumers Oil . . . . . . . . . . . . . . . . . . . . . . . . . . . . . . . . 90
    Revenue Ruling 60-275 . . . . . . . . . . . . . . . . . . . . . . . . . 91
    Weber . . . . . . . . . . . . . . . . . . . . . . . . . . . . . . . . . . . . . . 94
    Revenue Ruling 77-316 and the Service's Initial Victories . . 99
    Humana . . . . . . . . . . . . . . . . . . . . . . . . . . . . . . . . . . . 126
    Gulf Oil . . . . . . . . . . . . . . . . . . . . . . . . . . . . . . . . . . . 139
    Harper . . . . . . . . . . . . . . . . . . . . . . . . . . . . . . . . . . . . 146
    Sears . . . . . . . . . . . . . . . . . . . . . . . . . . . . . . . . . . . . . . 152
    Ocean Drilling . . . . . . . . . . . . . . . . . . . . . . . . . . . . . . 163
    Amerco . . . . . . . . . . . . . . . . . . . . . . . . . . . . . . . . . . . 170
    Malone and Hyde . . . . . . . . . . . . . . . . . . . . . . . . . . . . 174
    Kidde . . . . . . . . . . . . . . . . . . . . . . . . . . . . . . . . . . . . . 181
    UPS . . . . . . . . . . . . . . . . . . . . . . . . . . . . . . . . . . . . . . 189
    Revenue Ruling 2002-89 . . . . . . . . . . . . . . . . . . . . . . . 197
    Revenue Ruling 2002-90 . . . . . . . . . . . . . . . . . . . . . . . 201
    Revenue Ruling 2002-91 . . . . . . . . . . . . . . . . . . . . . . . 203
    Revenue Ruling 2005-40 . . . . . . . . . . . . . . . . . . . . . . . 206
    Revenue Ruling 2002-75 . . . . . . . . . . . . . . . . . . . . . . . 211
    Conclusion . . . . . . . . . . . . . . . . . . . . . . . . . . . . . . . . . 211

**Bibliography** . . . . . . . . . . . . . . . . . . . . . . . . . . . . . . . . . . 217

**Table of Cases** . . . . . . . . . . . . . . . . . . . . . . . . . . . . . . . . . 220

**Table of Statutes** . . . . . . . . . . . . . . . . . . . . . . . . . . . . . . . 224

# Introduction

I first encountered captive insurance in graduate school while attending the Thomas Jefferson School of Law. I was taking a course in offshore financial centers and had to read the *UPS* case—one of the last cases in the captive insurance cases (see part 2 of this book). In order to explain why this was a personal "light bulb" moment, you need to know two things from my background: before I went to law school, I was a bond broker, and at that job, I had insurance companies as clients. So, I knew the investment side of insurance companies. In addition, I've been blogging about economics for about four years at *The Bonddad Blog*. This means I'm familiar with insurance companies from their very important position as financial intermediaries in the financial system. So when I read the *UPS* case, several strands of thought came together into one conclusion: a business could form a financial intermediary. This is a truly extraordinary business opportunity for those who understand its consequences.

In the summer of 2009, I began to consider obtaining a doctorate in law and started looking at possible dissertation topics. Captive insurance wound up at the top of the list, so in the winter of 2008, I read a number of books and articles on the topic, in addition to the entire case law history of captives. That research not only forms the basis of my dissertation (which I am still writing) but also of this book.

This book has two purposes, the first of which is to provide the reader with a general overview of what I call the who, what, where, when, and why part of captive insurance. In other words, if you have heard about the concept of captive insurance and want to learn more, Part 1 is for you. It begins by answering the most basic question: who should form a captive insurance company? It is followed by a discussion of a captive's benefits. Following this general introduction, we start to discuss the nuts and bolts of captives with an explanation of the different types of captives and the overall corporate structures that can be used in a captive. The rest of the chapter is devoted to explaining the process of forming and running the captive. After reading Part 1, the reader should have the answer to many nuts and bolts questions.

Part 2 is a bit more complicated and scholarly. It is a case law history of captive insurance, from the reserve cases of the early 1900s to a series of revenue rulings written just after the turn of the century. I've included this section for lawyers (obviously) but also for people who are interested in the overall history of the legal arguments for and against captives that have been used over the last nearly one hundred years. Being a history buff, I think it is incredibly important for people to understand why captive insurance was the subject of litigation for a number of years—and also why the IRS finally threw in the towel and allowed captive insurance to continue.

# Part I: Captive Insurance Basics

**Who Should Form a Captive?**

While there is no firm answer to this question, the case law and a general review of available literature reveals the following trends.

A company that has an above-average risk profile should strongly consider forming a captive. The taxpayer in *Gulf Oil* was engaged in oil production.[1] Therefore, it was exposed to many types of high-risk activities such as oil drilling, transporting large amounts of flammable material, refining large quantities of flammable material, and handling numerous workers' compensation claims. As a result, Gulf found it difficult to find adequate insurance coverage.[2] The taxpayer in *Ocean Drilling* was engaged in offshore drilling—another high-risk business.[3] At the time of the case, offshore drilling was a new technology only insured by high-risk insurers such as Lloyd's of London.[4] Lloyd's continually increased the premiums it charged because it had little loss history on which

---

1    Gulf Oil v. C.I.R., 914 F.2d 396 (3rd Cir. 1990).
2    *Id.*
3    Ocean Drilling and Exploration Company v. United States, 988 F.2d 1135, 1138 (Fed. Cir. 1993).
4    Ocean Drilling and Exploration Company v. United States, 24 Cl. Ct. 714, 716 (1991).

to base its insurance rates.[5] Like the taxpayer in *Gulf Oil*, Ocean Drilling found it difficult to find cost-effective insurance.[6] The taxpayer in *Beech Aircraft* manufactured small airplanes.[7] The taxpayer in *Humana* was a large hospital chain.[8] The taxpayer in *Kidde* was exposed to product's liability risk.[9] All of these companies faced an above-average risk that in some way made it difficult to procure adequate insurance at affordable prices.

Anyone considering forming a captive should have a long-term horizon for the proper development and implementation of a captive program. The minimum time period should be seven years before reconsidering the decision to form the captive; ideally, it should be at least ten years. The primary reason for this is the importance of the time value of money and the captive's investment portfolio. If the insureds maintain a favorable loss profile—that is, the captive pays few claims—then the captive's investment portfolio will increase at strong rates thanks to the time value of money. For example, the Harper Group's captive saw its reserves for unexpired risk increase from $64,065 in 1974 to a little over $3 million in 1983.[10] This reserve could become a profit center for the parent or association group. However, it took over ten years for the Harper Group to develop that amount of money. In addition to the development of the investment portfolio is the possible implementation of a loss prevention program. This will lower

---

[5] *Id.*
[6] *Id.*
[7] Beech Aircraft v. United States, 1984 WL 988 at 1.
[8] Humana v. Commissioner, 88 T.C. 197, 199 (1987).
[9] Kidde Industries, Inc. v. United States, 40 Fed. Cl. 42, 45 (1997).
[10] The Harper Group and Includable Subsidiaries v. C.I.R., 96 T.C. 45, 53 (1991).

the claims the captive pays, thereby increasing the amount of money in the investment portfolio.

In addition, a company considering forming a captive must have the up-front financial resources to contribute to the captive. All US jurisdictions have minimum capital requirements for the captive, and all allow the insurance regulator to set the amount higher depending on the type and amount of insurance policies written by the captive. At minimum, the parent or participants should have $250,000 available in either cash or a line of credit. A higher contribution is likely.

There are no firm rules regarding the minimum amount of top-line revenue a company should have or the amount of annual insurance premiums a company should have. However, a good rule of thumb is that the prospective parent of a pure captive (see below) should have at least two of the following:

1.) at least $1.5 million in top-line revenue;
2.) $250,000 or more in "self-insured or uninsured business risk";
3.) one hundred or more employees; or
4.) $500,000 or more in annual commercial insurance expenses.[11]

## What Are the Benefits of a Captive Insurance Company?

There are many reasons why a company would choose to form a captive. Case law provides one of the most common reasons: a company is forced into creating its own captive because the

---

11   Taylor and Sobel, "Closer Look at Captive," CPA Journal, June 2008

insurance market no longer provides adequate coverage, or the private market only provides coverage at prohibitive prices. The plaintiff in *Consumer's Oil* owned property in a flood plain but could not find insurance.[12] The plaintiffs in *United States v. Weber* faced the exact same problem.[13] The plaintiff in *Ocean Drilling* was an offshore oil company that could not find adequate insurance for its offshore activities.[14] The plaintiff in *Humana* was a large, nationally known hospital chain that almost went without insurance because of the cost.[15] In all of the preceding cases, the private market did not provide the plaintiffs with the coverage they needed; hence, all the companies were forced to create their own captives.

A second reason for creating a captive is to obtain more control over the insurance policy. Case law provides a classic example: in *Beech Aircraft*, the plaintiff wanted an insurance policy where the company had more control over the attorneys during litigation.[16] The company lost a large tort claim, which the company felt was caused by its attorneys, who were appointed by its insurer.[17] The company went so far as to try to have its insurance company–appointed counsel removed during trial.[18] Beech needed an insurance policy that gave it far more control over the attorneys appointed in case of a claim. This leads to two reasons for forming a captive insurance company.

---

12  Consumers Oil Corporation of Trenton v. United States, 166 F. Supp. 796, 797–98 (New Jersey 1960).
13  United States v. Weber Paper Company, 320 F.2d 199, 201 (8th Cir. 1963).
14  *Ocean*, 988 F.2d 1135, 1138.
15  *Humana,* 88 T.C. 197, 200.
16  *Beech Aircraft*, 1984 WL 988 at 1.
17  *Id.*
18  *Id.*

First, you can create whatever type of coverage for the operating business that you can dream up. Second, you can draft the policies according to whatever terms you desire. The only limit to these two advantages is that they must fall within the minimal bounds of commercial reasonableness.[19]

The book goes on to list over seventy types of insurance that can be written by a captive ranging from standard policies, such as malpractice[20] and errors and omissions,[21] to more esoteric policies, such as weather[22] and business extortion.[23]

As a corollary to the above rule,

> [a captive insured can get b]etter service for [its] insurance exposure. A captive can tailor its insurance program to meets its own specific situation. This can involve better loss control, better underwriting and more control over the handling and settlement of claims.[24]

In conjunction with establishing its own captive, the insured can undertake a comprehensive risk-reduction program. This will help to lower their overall insurance premiums after implementation, because the plan should lower the amount of claims paid by the captive.

---

19  Adkisson, *Captive Insurance Companies*, 56.
20  *Id.* at 59.
21  *Id.*
22  *Id.* at 67.
23  *Id.* at 61.
24  Captive FAQs, Milliman, available at http://www.captive.com/service/milliman/faq.shtml.

A third reason for forming a captive is cost reduction:

> A corporation paying an insurance premium to a conventional insurance company contributes to the expenses of [that] insurer (including inefficient administration and other insureds' losses) and profits of the insurer. By establishing one's own insurance vehicle, such costs and profits [become] subject to control within the same economic family.[25]

For example, in the second quarter of 2009, the Traveler's Insurance Company had selling, general, and administrative expenses of $839 billion.[26] Over the same period, Aetna had selling, general, and administrative expenses of $1.4 billion.[27] To a certain extent, each company's premiums reflect these costs. Compare that to a captive that has little selling and marketing expense because it is dealing with a limited number of insureds. This lowers the cost of insurance issued by the captive.

Fourth, the insured should be able to increase the corporate family's cash flow.[28] Under a traditional insurance scheme using a third-party insurer, the insured makes the insurance payment

---

[25] Why Form a Captive? Alta Holdings LLC, available at http://www.altaholdings.com/why-form-captives/default.aspx.

[26] Available from information obtained on Google Finance, available at http://www.google.com/finance?q=NYSE:TRV&fstype=ii.

[27] Available from information obtained on Google Finance, available at http://www.google.com/finance?q=NYSE:AET&fstype=ii.

[28] Why Form a Captive? Alta Holdings LLC, available at http://www.altaholdings.com/why-form-captives/default.aspx; see also Captive FAQs, Milliman, available at http://www.captive.com/service/milliman/faq.shtml.

to the third-party insurer, at which time the payment leaves the insured's economic family. However, when the insured owns the insurance company, the payment stays within the same corporate family. This still allows the insured to deduct the insurance payment as a legitimate business expense.[29] However, the insurance premium is gross income to the captive.[30] If the parent and captive elect to file as an affiliated group,[31] the premium becomes part of the affiliated group's income.[32] Compare this to the traditional method of insurance, where an independent third party would keep the payment and invest the non-paid claims

---

29  26 U.S.C. 162(a).

30  26 U.S.C. 832(b)(1)(A).

31  26 U.S.C. 1504: "The term 'affiliated group' means– (A) 1 or more chains of includible corporations connected through stock ownership with a common parent corporation which is an includible corporation, but only if - (B)(i) the common parent owns directly stock meeting the requirements of paragraph (2) in at least 1 of the other includible corporations, and (ii) stock meeting the requirements of paragraph (2) in each of the includible corporations (except the common parent) is owned directly by 1 or more of the other includible corporations. (2) 80%0% voting and value test. The ownership of stock of any corporation meets the requirements of this paragraph if it - (A) possesses at least 80% of the total voting power of the stock of such corporation, and (B) has a value equal to at least 80% of the total value of the stock of such corporation."

32  26 U.S.C. 1501: "An affiliated group of corporations shall, subject to the provisions of this chapter, have the privilege of making a consolidated return with respect to the income tax imposed by chapter 1 for the taxable year in lieu of separate returns. The making of a consolidated return shall be upon the condition that all corporations which at any time during the taxable year have been members of the affiliated group consent to all the consolidated return regulations prescribed under section 1502 prior to the last day prescribed by law for the filing of such return. The making of a consolidated return shall be considered as such consent. In the case of a corporation which is a member of the affiliated group for a fractional part of the year, the consolidated return shall include the income of such corporation for such part of the year as it is a member of the affiliated group."

into its own portfolio, which would then benefit the insurance company but not the company paying the premium.

Fifth, the insured can use its own loss experience in determining insurance rates.[33] While underwriters used to consider each insured's unique loss experience, that situation rarely exists now.[34] If the parent has a good loss profile, the captive can use this in determining premiums. As a result, the captive will allow the insured to tailor the insurance policy specifically to the insured's unique loss experience.

Sixth, captives can be used as wealth transfer vehicles.[35] Here is the general plan. A company owned by a high net worth individual establishes a captive.[36] The captive has written premiums higher than $350,000 and lower than $1.2 million.[37] As a result, the captive is taxed on its taxable investment income, which is usually lower than net premiums received.[38] At the same time, the estate's beneficiaries are shareholders of the captive.[39]

---

33 Adkisson, *Captive Insurance Companies*, 4.
34 *Id.*
35 Wealth Management Solutions, LLC, Estate Planning With a Captive Insurance Company, available at, Ihttp://www.wmsolutionsnow.com/estate_planning_with_a_captive_insurance_company.htm.
36 *Id.*
37 26 U.S.C. 831(b)(2)(A)(i) states, "In lieu of the tax otherwise applicable under subsection (a), there is hereby imposed for each taxable year on the income of every insurance company to which this subsection applies a tax computed by multiplying the taxable investment income of such company for such taxable year by the rates provided in section 11(b) ... This subsection shall apply to every insurance company other than life (including interinsurers and reciprocal underwriters) if– (i) the net written premiums (or, if greater, direct written premiums) for the taxable year exceed $350,000 but do not exceed $1,200,000."
38 *Id.*
39 *Id.*

It is best if they own the captive through a trust to protect the shares from future creditors' claims.[40] The children receive the benefit of increased share prices caused by an increase in the captive's overall net worth. However, the captive is subject to a lower level of taxation because of the 831(b) exception. Because of certain tax attributes of insurance companies (such as the ability to deduct contributions to reserves from its gross income), the captive can act as a wealth accumulation vehicle.[41]

Seventh, owning a captive gives the owner direct access to the reinsurance market.[42] Reinsurers usually have lower costs of operation and regulatory barriers,[43] along with lower administration expenses.[44] This spares the captive the cost of insurance mark-ups.[45] However, most reinsurers are only interested in large premiums,[46] thereby preventing the smaller captive from meaningfully participating in the reinsurance market.

Eighth, a captive can provide the insureds with a negotiation tool when dealing with other insurers.[47] The reasoning is

---

40  Adkisson, *Captive Insurance Companies*, 12.
41  *Id.* at 13.
42  Captive.com, Nine Reasons For Forming a Captive Insurance Company, available at, http://captive.com/newsstand/articles/5.html.
43  Theriault, *What to Consider When Establishing*.
44  Adkisson, *Captive Insurance Companies*, 7.
45  Captives.com, Captives, Why or Why Not, available at http://captive.com/service/SCG/ProsAndCons.html.
46  Adkisson, *Captive Insurance Companies*, 7: "A caveat here is that reinsurance companies will only participate in risks where significant premiums will be paid for the reinsurance coverage ... Few if any reinsurance companies will be interested in less than a six-figure reinsurance premium and many will not be interested until the premiums are in the seven or eight figure range."
47  Theriault, *What to Consider When Establishing*.

simple: when the insured has a captive, he or she is not in dire need of insurance. Instead, he or she may be able to take or leave the policy provided by an independent third-party insurer. This changes the dynamic of a negotiation, giving the insured more leverage when dealing with an insurer.

Ninth, a captive can provide stable pricing.[48] If the insured already has a good loss history—or if the insured develops and successfully implements a comprehensive loss program in conjunction with forming the captive—the loss experience can be reflected in the captive's premiums. In contrast, insurance provided by a third-party insurer places the insured at the whims of similar insureds covered by the insurer.

## What Type of Captive Should a Company Form?

A pure captive "insures risks of its parent and affiliated companies or controlled unaffiliated business."[49] Some states do not allow the pure captive to insure unaffiliated businesses.[50] Because of the limited pool of possible insureds, a pure captive can only be created by a company that has the financial resources to contribute all of the original capital to the captive.

Insurance Company Captives

For an insurance company that wants to form a captive, there are two options. The first is to form a branch captive, which is usually defined as "any alien captive insurer licensed by the

---

48   Captives.com, Captives, Why or Why Not, available at http://captive.com/service/SCG/ProsAndCons.html.
49   Vt. Stat. An. Tit. 8 Section 6001(14).
50   S.D. Codified Laws Section 58-46-1(5).

Commissioner to transact the business of insurance in the [jurisdiction] through a business unit with a principal place of business in the [jurisdiction]."[51] In other words, branch captives are only available to captive insurance companies licensed in other states. In comparison, an agency captive is "a captive insurer that is owned by an insurance agency or brokerage and that only insures risks of policies which are placed by or though the agency or brokerage."[52] In other words, the agency captive is a formal business entity in another jurisdiction that only deals with a licensed insurance company or agent in another jurisdiction.

Group Captives

There are several types of captives that underwrite group risks.

An association captive "insures risks of the member organizations of the association."[53] Most jurisdictions allow the captive to insure the risks of the members' affiliated

---

51  D.C. Code Ann. Section 31-3931.01(7); see also Mont. Code Ann. Section 33-28-101(5): "[a branch captive] is any foreign captive insurance company licensed by the commissioner to transact the business of insurance in this state through a business unit with a principal place of business in this state."

52  Nev. Rev. Stat. 694C.030; see also Ariz. Rev. Stat. Section 20-1098(2): "owned by one or more business entities that are licensed in any state as insurance producers or managing general agents and that only insure risks on policies placed through their owners."; D.C. Code Ann. Section 31-3931.01(2): "a captive insurer that is owned by an insurance agency or brokerage and that only insures risks of policies that are placed by or through the agency or brokerage."

53  Vt. Stat. Ann. Tit. 8, Section 6001(3); see also Haw. Rev. Stat. Section 431:19-101, S.C. Code Ann. Section 38-90-10(4), Del. Stat. Ann. tit. 18, section 6902(4).

companies.[54] The general definition of association is found in South Carolina's captive insurance law: An association is a group of business entities, political subdivisions, or individuals who have associated for at least a year.

  (a) the member organizations of which collectively, or which does itself:
      (i) own, control, or hold with power to vote all of the outstanding voting securities of an association captive insurance company incorporated as a stock insurer or organized as a limited liability company; or
      (ii) have complete voting control over an association captive insurance company organized as a mutual insurer; or
  (b) the member organizations of which collectively constitute all of the subscribers of an association captive insurance company formed as a reciprocal insurer.[55]

An association comprised of individuals is usually formed "to increase the members' buying power,"[56] whereas an association of businesses is usually formed "to obtain insurance that is otherwise unobtainable in the open market or is overpriced."[57] From a structuring perspective, note the insureds are also the captive owners. This creates important structuring issues. In an association formed as a stock insurer, a member's proposed

---

54 Del. Stat. Ann. tit. 18, section 6902(4), KY. Rev. Stat. Ann Section 304.49-010(5), Me. Rev. Stat. Ann. Tit. 24-A, Section 6701(3).
55 S.C. Code Ann. Section 38-90-10(3).
56 Adkisson, *Captive Insurance Companies*, 31.
57 *Id.*

leaving may create issues related to corporate governance, risk distribution, and possibly the overall viability of the captive. For example, suppose a member of an association captive owns 20 percent of the captive and is the largest insured. Now suppose that company is purchased by a much larger company that has its own insurance arrangement, meaning it does not need to participate in the association captive. The loss of 20 percent may threaten the captive's very existence. At minimum, it will raise problems that must be dealt with quickly, thereby taking important time away from other association members. A second and related issue is that—unlike subsidiaries of a pure captive—members of the association captive are not related through interlocking corporate directories. As such, there is less decision-making cohesion at the board of directors/upper management level of the captive. This can create unwanted friction for the captive and must be considered and dealt with when forming the captive.

Risk Retention Groups

Risk retention groups (RRGs) were originally conceived of under the Products Liability Risk Retention Act of 1981.[58] Congress passed the law "because of the lack of product liability insurance at affordable rates."[59] As such, one of the primary reasons for passing the act was to "increase the availability of coverage by promoting greater competition in the insurance industry,"[60] thereby lowering insurance rates.[61] The Liability Risk Prevention Act of 1986 broadened the scope of this law to include professional groups

---

58  44 C.J.S. Insurance Section 52.
59  *Id.*
60  43 Am. Jur. 2d Insurance Section 29.
61  44 C.J.S. Insurance Section 52.

such as health care providers.[62] In essence, this law allows groups of professionals to form their own insurance company.

A risk retention group is "any corporation or other limited liability association"[63] that is organized[64] for the "primary activity ... of assuming, and spreading all, or any portion, of the liability exposure of its group members."[65] All "members are engaged in businesses or activities similar or related with respect to the liability to which such members are exposed by virtue of any related, similar, or common business, trade, product, services, premises, or operations."[66] Members cannot be excluded solely to provide members of the RRG a competitive advantage over the excluded person or company.[67] The group

> (i) has as its owners only persons who comprise the membership of the risk retention group and who are provided insurance by such group; or
> (ii) has as its sole owner an organization which has as—
> > (I) its members only persons who comprise the membership of the risk retention group; and
> > (II) its owners only persons who comprise the membership of the risk retention group and who are provided insurance by such group.[68]

---

62  44 C.J.S. Insurance Section 52.
63  15 U.S.C. 3901(a)(4).
64  15 U.S.C. 3901(a)(4)(B).
65  15 U.S.C. 3901(a)(4)(A).
66  15 U.S.C. 3901(a)(4)(F).
67  15 U.S.C. 3901(a)(4)(D).
68  15 U.S.C. 3901(a)(4)(E).

With a few exceptions,[69] states are prohibited from regulating RRGs.

---

69 See 15 U.S.C. 3902(1): "(1) make unlawful, or regulate, directly or indirectly, the operation of a risk retention group except that the jurisdiction in which it is chartered may regulate the formation and operation of such a group and any State may require such a group to— (A) comply with the unfair claim settlement practices law of the State; (B) pay, on a nondiscriminatory basis, applicable premium and other taxes which are levied on admitted insurers and surplus lines insurers, brokers, or policyholders under the laws of the State; (C) participate, on a nondiscriminatory basis, in any mechanism established or authorized under the law of the State for the equitable apportionment among insurers of liability insurance losses and expenses incurred on policies written through such mechanism; (D) register with and designate the State insurance commissioner as its agent solely for the purpose of receiving service of legal documents or process; (E) submit to an examination by the State insurance commissioners in any State in which the group is doing business to determine the group's financial condition, if— (i) the commissioner of the jurisdiction in which the group is chartered has not begun or has refused to initiate an examination of the group; and (ii) any such examination shall be coordinated to avoid unjustified duplication and unjustified repetition; (F) comply with a lawful order issued— (i) in a delinquency proceeding commenced by the State insurance commissioner if there has been a finding of financial impairment under subparagraph (E); or (ii) in a voluntary dissolution proceeding; (G) comply with any State law regarding deceptive, false, or fraudulent acts or practices, except that if the State seeks an injunction regarding the conduct described in this subparagraph, such injunction must be obtained from a court of competent jurisdiction; (H) comply with an injunction issued by a court of competent jurisdiction, upon a petition by the State insurance commissioner alleging that the group is in hazardous financial condition or is financially impaired; and (I) provide the following notice, in 10-point type, in any insurance policy issued by such group: 'This policy is issued by your risk retention group. Your risk retention group may not be subject to all of the insurance laws and regulations of your State. State insurance insolvency guaranty funds are not available for your risk retention group.' (2) require or permit a risk retention group to participate in any insurance insolvency guaranty association to which an insurer licensed in the State is required to belong; (3) require any insurance policy issued to a risk retention group or any

In addition to a risk retention group is a purchasing group, which is defined under federal law as a group that

(A) has as one of its purposes the purchase of liability insurance on a group basis;
(B) purchases such insurance only for its group members and only to cover their similar or related liability exposure, as described in subparagraph (C);
(C) is composed of members whose businesses or activities are similar or related with respect to the liability to which members are exposed by virtue of any related, similar, or common business, trade, product, services, premises, or operations; and
(D) is domiciled in any State.[70]

In other words, a purchasing group acts as an agent for a group of similarly situated companies who share the same risk profile. This is in contrast to the risk retention group that formally underwrites the risks of the group's members.

Another type of group captive is an industrial insured captive insurer, which insures the risk for an industrial insurance group, and which usually has criteria similar to the following:

a. Any group of industrial insureds that collectively meet any of the following criteria:

---

member of the group to be countersigned by an insurance agent or broker residing in that State; or (4) otherwise, discriminate against a risk retention group or any of its members, except that nothing in this section shall be construed to affect the applicability of State laws generally applicable to persons or corporations.".

[70] 15 U.S.C. 3901(a)(5).

1. Own, control, or hold with power to vote all of the outstanding voting securities of an industrial insured captive insurance company incorporated as a stock insurer.
2. Have complete voting control over an industrial insured captive insurance company incorporated as a mutual insurer.
3. Constitute all of the subscribers of an industrial insured captive insurance company formed as a reciprocal insurer.

b. Any group which is created under the Product Liability Risk Retention Act of 1981, 15 U.S. Code § 3901 et seq., as amended, as a corporation or other limited liability association taxable as a stock insurance company or a mutual insurer [this is a risk retention group, which is explained above].[71]

An industrial insured traditionally occurs where the "insured has total aggregate insurance premiums over $25,000,[72] 25 or more employees[73] and a full-time employee acting as an insurance manager or buyer."[74]

Special Category Captives

There are two types of captives that do not fall into convenient categories. The first is a "rent-a-captive," also called a "segregated cell captive" or "sponsored cell company."

---

71  Ala. Code Section 27-31B-2(14).
72  Vt. Stat. Ann. Tit. 8, Section 6001(8)(B).
73  Vt. Stat. Ann. Tit. 8, Section 6001(8)(C).
74  Vt. Stat. Ann. Tit. 8, Section 8001(8)(A).

The rent-a-captive simply involves an insurance company that accepts the insured's risk, provides capital to back the risk, and then pays the insured a percentage of the underwriting profits or charges the insured for underwriting losses.[75]

Each insured's risk is segregated into a cell, which is a/are

> separate account(s) established by a sponsored captive insurance company formed or licensed under the provisions of [the respective captive code], in which assets are maintained for one or more participants in accordance with the terms of one or more participant contracts to fund the liability of the sponsored captive insurance company assumed on behalf of such participants as set forth in such participant contracts.[76]

Conceptually, rent-a-captives are like honeycombs, where risks are placed in a separate account completely segregated in all ways from other cells.[77] While many jurisdictions have these structures, they are somewhat untested: "nobody really knows

---

[75] Adkisson, *Captive Insurance Companies*, 32; see also Vt. Stat. Ann. tit. 8, Section 6032(3): "a separate account established by a sponsored captive insurance company formed or licensed under the provisions of this chapter, in which assets are maintained for one or more participants in accordance with the terms of one or more participant contracts to fund the liability of the sponsored captive insurance company assumed on behalf of such participants as set forth in such participant contracts."

[76] Vt. Stat. Ann. Tit. 8, Section 6032(3).

[77] Adkisson, *Captive Insurance Companies*, 33.

how well a rent-a-captive structure will stand up for U.S. tax purposes as to the deductibility of premiums paid."[78]

A special purpose financial captive (SPFC) is organized "for the exclusive purpose of facilitating the securitization of one or more risks as a means of accessing alternative sources of capital and achieving the benefits of securitization."[79] More specifically,

> SPFCs are created for the limited purpose of entering into an SPFC contract and insurance securitization transactions and into related agreements to facilitate the accomplishment and execution of those transactions. The creation of SPFCs is intended to achieve greater efficiencies in structuring and executing insurance securitizations, to diversify and broaden insurers' access to sources of capital, to facilitate access for many insurers to insurance securitization and capital markets financing technology.[80]

In general, an SPFC takes on a risk through an insurance or reinsurance contract and then funds that risk through securities markets. While this broadens the risk pool that can be accessed, it also increases compliance costs because the issuance of securities adds SEC compliance to the captive's compliance cost.

---

78  Adkisson, *Captive Insurance Companies*, 33.
79  Haw. Rev. Stat. Section 431:19-201.
80  S.C. Code Ann. Section 38-90-410.

## What Type of Corporate Structure Should I Use?

Most statutes specifically dictate what corporate form a certain type of captive may assume. For example, a statute may state that a pure captive can only be a stock insurer. Therefore, the type of captive insurer picked by the people or company forming the captive will usually dictate the type of company formed or the range of corporate structures that are possible. Additionally—and just as importantly—most state statutes require that the insureds also be the captive's owners. Because of the corporate duties imposed on a company's board of directors (see discussion below), this could complicate the operation of either the insured or insurer if handled incorrectly. Finally, under federal law, all insurance companies are considered corporations, or C-Corps. This does not make the form meaningless. For example, LLCs typically have a far lower number of affirmative duties to perform under the governing statute, making them a very attractive business choice.

A stock insurer is owned by shareholders.[81] Each state has an individual corporate code, which governs the formation, operation, and winding up of each company's affairs. Formation is accomplished by filing a charter or the articles of incorporation with the respective secretary of state.[82] Usually, the articles of incorporation or charter will contain the company's name, its purpose, and details about its initial capitalization (the amount of stock, the type of stock, and par value), the name and address of the corporation's authorized agent, and the initial board of directors.[83] After formal incorporation, the

---

81   3 Couch on Insurance Section 39:3.
82   CJS Corporations Section 48.
83   Emanuel, *Corporations*, 15.

company must adopt bylaws, which govern the company's internal affairs.[84]

Stockholders control the selection of officers and directors, which is accomplished by voting.[85] Stock companies are run by stockholders who must hold regular meetings.[86] The regularity of their meetings is defined by statute or more specifically the corporation's bylaws—but it is traditionally at least once per year.[87] Decisions must be "based upon deliberate conference and intelligent discussion of proposed measures."[88] The decisions of the corporation are based on the voting rights inherent to that ownership interest.[89] The method of voting is specifically spelled out in the corporation's bylaws.[90]

The board of directors is responsible for the overall corporate direction—they run the corporation's affairs.[91] The officers such as the president and vice president are charged with carrying out the day-to-day affairs of the corporation.[92] Directors and officers are subject to three important rules. The first is the duty of care, which states that the officer or director must "be diligent in respect of the management and administration of the affairs of the corporation and in the use or preservation of its property and assets."[93] Failure to adhere to this rule leads to

---

84  *Id.*
85  3 Couch on Insurance Section 39:5.
86  Amjur Corporations Section 789.
87  Amjur Corporations Section 779.
88  Amjur Corporations Section 789.
89  Amjur Corporations Section 850.
90  *Id.*
91  CJS Corporations Section 543.
92  CJS Corporations Section 553.
93  Amjur Corporations Section 1465.

personal liability for the director or officer for damages to the corporation.[94] Second, the business judgment rule is based on the following five points:

(1) the management of a corporation's affairs is placed by law in the hands of its board of directors;
(2) the performance of the directors' management function consists of decision making, that is, the making of economic choices and the weighing of the potential of risk against the potential of reward, and supervision of officers and employees, that is, attentiveness to corporate affairs;
(3) corporate directors are not guarantors of the financial success of their management efforts;
(4) though not guarantors, directors as fiduciaries should be held legally accountable to the corporation and its stockholders when their performance falls short of meeting appropriate standards; and
(5) such culpability occurs when directors breach their fiduciary duty, that is, when they breach the duty of loyalty by profiting improperly from their positions or breach the duty of care by failing to supervise corporate affairs with the appropriate level of skill.[95]

The business judgment rule assumes that when a director or officer makes an informed decision in good faith, he or she will be insulated from any negative consequences of his or her decisions. For example, if a director analyzes all available facts and makes a decision that is unprofitable, the director is

---

94   *Id.*
95   Amjur Corporations Section 1470.

insulated from liability for that decision.[96] Finally, directors owe a duty of loyalty to the corporation, which prevents self-dealing.[97] This duty "requires that a corporation receive the full benefit of transactions in which the officer engages on the corporation's behalf, without thought to personal gain."[98]

"Mutual insurance ... exists where several persons have joined together for their united protection, each member contributing to a fund for the payment of the losses and expenses."[99] The earnings of the company—over and above the payments of the losses, operating expenses, and reserves—are the property of the policyholders.[100] There are two types of mutual insurance companies. An advance premium mutual "collect[s] most or all of the cost of the insurance at the time the contract is written."[101] These are by far the predominant type of mutual.[102] In contrast, "assessable mutuals are companies that charge an initial fixed premium and, if that isn't sufficient, might further assess policyholders to meet losses in excess of the premiums that have been charged."[103] Assessable mutuals write insurance primarily on fire and windstorm policies for farms and small town dwellings.[104] Members of assessable mutuals are subject to two types of possible future charges. An unlimited liability

---

96  *Id.*
97  Amjur Corporations Section 1480.
98  *Id.*
99  3 Couch on Insurance Section 39:15.
100 A.M. Best, Glossary of Insurance Terms, available at http://www.ambest.com/resource/glossary.html#M.
101 3 Couch on Insurance Section 39:16.
102 *Id.*
103 A.M. Best, Glossary of Insurance Terms, available at http://www.ambest.com/resource/glossary.html#M.
104 3 Couch on Insurance Section 39:17.

plan means that a member "is bound to pay a proportional share of all losses and legitimate expenses of the company."[105] The other is a limited liability mutual where the members are limited by a specific dollar amount or a multiple of their premium.[106]

Mutuals are usually required to incorporate formally and are therefore subject to a specific jurisdiction's corporate code.[107] Where not required to incorporate formally, they are subject to partnership laws.[108] Mutual policyholders are the equivalent of shareholders.[109] "They participate in the operation of the mutual through voting rights."[110] Directors and officers of mutuals are generally bound to the same rules and duties of similar members of business corporations (see discussion above).[111]

> A reciprocal or inter-insurance exchange is an aggregation of persons, called subscribers, who, through an attorney-in-fact, cooperate to furnish themselves and each other insurance against a designated risk, and the subscribers are both the insured and the insurers.[112]

---

105 3 Couch on Insurance Section 39:17.
106 *Id.*
107 CJS Insurance Section 172.
108 *Id.*
109 3 Couch on Insurance Section 39:15.
110 *Id.*
111 3 Couch on Insurance Section 39:22.
112 3 Couch on Insurance Section 39:48.

In a reciprocal, the insured is also the insurer.[113] A reciprocal arrangement eliminates the "part of the insurance premium that ordinarily goes to profit."[114] Unlike a mutual, a reciprocal insurer is not incorporated.[115] An attorney-in-fact acts as the middleman for those participating, issuing contracts "to and for the subscribers."[116] Each subscriber signs a power of attorney in favor of the attorney-in-fact, which grants the attorney-in-fact his or her specific powers as they relate to the exchange.[117] Each subscriber's premium is directly related to the amount of insurance he or she is providing to the other subscribers.[118] Subscribers to the exchange have a contingent liability to the exchange "subject to any valid limitation ... to pay an amount sufficient to satisfy creditors to the exchange."[119]

**How to Form a Captive**

**Domicile Selection**

The book *Captives and the Management of Risk* uses the acronym "TRIP" to describe the four primary considerations for domicile selection: taxes, regulation, infrastructure, and perception.[120] I would add geography (changing the acronym to GRIPT) for the following reason. There are numerous states that have captive insurance statutes. Because most statutes require the insureds also to be captive owners, forming a captive

---

113 *Id.*
114 *Id.*
115 *Id.*
116 3 Couch on Insurance Section 39:53.
117 3 Couch on Insurance Section 39:53.
118 3 Couch on Insurance Section 39:55.
119 3 Couch on Insurance Section 39:56.
120 Westover, *Captives and the Management*, chapter 11.

creates additional corporate leadership responsibilities for the insureds. For example, most jurisdictions require the captive to have at least one meeting per year within the jurisdiction, along with a registered agent and physical address. Additionally, most jurisdictions require at least one person forming the captive to be from the state. While it may be attractive to form a captive in a more exotic jurisdiction, it can also increase compliance costs. For example, suppose there is a problem with the captive that requires in-person problem solving. The choice of a Caribbean location for a company on the West Coast would greatly increase compliance costs. In contrast, if the same company formed a captive in Utah, Nevada, or Arizona (or perhaps Hawaii), it would be far easier and cheaper to fly to the jurisdiction to deal with the problem. Also of importance, many US states in non-exotic jurisdictions, such as South Dakota, Kentucky, and Kansas, now have captive statutes—most likely to keep their respective state businesses from forming a captive outside the state. Simply put, it may be possible for a company to form a captive in its state of origin or a neighboring state. While this may decrease the attractiveness from an annual meeting perspective, it may significantly decrease compliance costs.

"Regulations" are not a dry analysis of the rules associated with a particular jurisdiction. Instead, regulations refer to "why one or another domicile might make it easier for the shareholder or insured to achieve its risk financing objectives."[121] This criteria looks at how each state implements its respective captive regulations. There are four different types of methods. The first is regulation by ratio, whereby the captive must simply

---

121 Westover, *Captives and the Management*, chapter 11.

maintain certain financial ratios.[122] This is an easy, hands-off approach to overseeing a captive that has a low compliance cost.[123] The second method is the "plan of operations" method, whereby the captive files a plan of operations (how it will go about its business), and the captive managers inform the regulator when they deviate from the plan.[124] This method may give the state the right to veto any change in operation that the regulator believes will endanger the captive's viability.[125] The third method is "regulation by examination," whereby the insurance commissioner will perform an on-site examination on a regular or semi-regular basis.[126] This is the method favored by US jurisdictions. This can increase compliance costs, as regulators must be paid for.[127] This goal is usually accomplished through taxation.[128] The fourth type of regulatory scheme is

> to define and monitor the financial net worth and sophistication of the captive shareholder and insureds, rather than require detailed information about the captive. Regulatory focus on the financial strength of captive users is a natural result of the fact that commercial insurance regulations are slowly moving toward less regulation for large commercial buyers, recognizing that the sophistication of their risk financing activities requires a different type of surveillance. The key for efficient captive regulation is

---

122  *Id.*
123  *Id.*
124  *Id.*
125  *Id.*
126  *Id.*
127  *Id.*
128  *Id.*

to determine which captive owners and insureds need regulatory oversight and which don't.[129]

"Infrastructure" refers to the state of the captive industry within a particular jurisdiction.[130] For example, most jurisdictions require a captive to utilize an "approved" manager. How large is the list of "approved" managers for the jurisdiction? How easy is it to get another manager approved? How broad are the services offered within the jurisdiction? These are questions that must be answered on a jurisdiction-by-jurisdiction basis.

Perception is the factor most difficult to explain.[131] However, it is based on aligning the parent's corporate culture with the jurisdiction most likely to jibe with the parent's corporate culture.[132] The captive planner will need to know about the parent's financial and operating profile to make this determination.

Finally, there are taxes. Some jurisdictions do not tax captives in any way.[133] Others have caps on the maximum rate of tax that can be charged,[134] while others have no maximum tax rate.[135] Federal tax issues are dealt with under the taxation section of running a captive.

---

129  *Id.*
130  *Id.*
131  *Id.*
132  *Id.*
133  For example, Utah and Arizona
134  D.C. Code Ann. Section 31-3931.12(e).
135  Ark. Code Ann. Section 23-63-1614(c).

**Feasibility Study**

The first practical step in forming a captive is to perform a feasibility study. While there are legitimate reasons not to take this step,[136] the benefits are simply too great to ignore. One of the primary benefits of a feasibility study is that it "allows captive users to realistically assess and understand their expected return on investment."[137] In other words, it allows the insureds to make an informed decision based on independently prepared and analyzed financial information. It is important to remember that the insureds are forming an insurance company. This is a unique business structure that the insureds probably have little knowledge about. The feasibility study can help to educate the insureds on the practical day-to-day procedures and requirements of running an insurance company. In addition, the study "helps a firm assess the benefits and costs associated with a captive compared to other risk-financing alternatives."[138] As such, the report's value far outweighs any drawbacks.

The feasibility study has three objectives. First, it aids in compliance.[139] Forming an insurance company involves several different statutes: the insurance and corporate code of the jurisdiction where the captive is formed and federal tax issues. These legal issues must be dealt with in an organized

---

136 See Westover, *Captive Practices and Procedures*, 4–6. (To maintain confidentiality regarding sensitive corporate/company information, the prospect is a high net worth individual/company who inherently understands the risks and rewards, or the promoter has already established similar captives numerous times.)
137 *Id.* at 6.
138 Moody, "Actuarial Involvement in Captive Formations."
139 *Id.* at 7.

and disciplined way. Second, the study provides education on the captive and the overall program objectives.[140] While the people advocating the program will obviously understand the important benefits and nuances of the program, others will not. The study helps to provide those unfamiliar with captive insurance the necessary knowledge to make an informed opinion. Third—and in correlation to the previous point—the study can aid in selling important decision-makers within the organization on the plan.[141]

> The risk manager may have already determined that [the captive] is the best way for dealing with a specific coverage or capacity issue, but without a formal feasibility study it will be hard to persuade the organization to commit capital and resources to the project.[142]

A company will need to provide the following items and information for the feasibility study:

  i.   Exposure values, current and projected (payroll, revenue, vehicles, property values, and locations)
  ii.  5 years' prior loss history (incurred or paid basis), by line of business
  iii. Annual report or financial statements of insured
  iv.  Copies of current policies
  v.   Premium and claims services payment schedule.[143]

---

140  *Id.* at 8.
141  *Id.*
142  *Id.*
143  Westover, *Captives and the Management*, chapter 11, exhibit 11.1.

This information is then analyzed, with the final data becoming part of the feasibility study. The study will eventually have four sections:

(1) A background and scope of the analysis, which provides a "summary of coverage, policy forms, lines of business, limits' deductibles, and retentions"[144] and a "summary of the source of funds."[145]
(2) A summary of recommendations, which includes information on the different lines of insurance offered along with the rate structure and premiums associated with each individual line of insurance.[146]
(3) An analysis section that includes the following:
    1. ... [S]tudies based on estimates of expected frequency and severity of loss using available data. These estimates may be derived from: trended and developed historical loss data; outside sources of data (ISO, RAA, etc.); expertise within the firm; and judgment. It should be noted, however, that judgmental estimates should be disclosed as such and the source clearly stated. Judgmental estimates may be accepted as long as they are clearly disclosed.
    2. Loss projections and risk margins of expected and higher-than-expected levels of loss ... These projections and margins are either actuarially determined and stated as such or the methodology used is clearly documented. In all loss projection

---

144 *Id.*
145 *Id.*
146 *Id.*

sections, each step should be explained in terms of how and why the procedure was used. For example, how is trend and loss development handled? Are losses discounted for the time value of money?
3. [A clear discussion of the e]xpense budget for the captive insurance company . In addition, the CICFS must make reference to tax issues. The tax issues should address, either the state that the captive insurance company is subject to within the models, or that the captive insurance company is not subject to tax consequences. Should the CICFS state that the captive insurance company is not subject to taxes of certain jurisdictions the reasons for this must be clearly documented. The Bureau considers tax consequences to be an extremely important consideration of captive insurance company formation. Types of tax issues may include but are not limited to the following:

    U.S. Income tax—to the captive, to the owners
    Excise taxes
    Excess and surplus lines taxes
    Domicile premiums taxes
    Local premium taxes
    Other assessments or applicable taxes (i.e. residual market mechanisms)
4. Premiums/Funding [for] items (2) and (3) should be brought together in order to develop the total recommended premium for the captive.

5. Capitalization ... to cover the variability and uncertainty of expected loss levels. Therefore, a relatively extensive discussion of capitalization should be included in the CICFS. Included in the discussion should be a review of minimum participation requirements and any heuristic logic used in determining capitalization.[147]

(4) Pro forma financial statements.[148]

From a legal/regulatory standpoint, the feasibility study must discuss the issue of insurance regulation and its effect on running the captive. The passage of the McCarran-Ferguson Act relegated insurance regulation to the states.[149] The key phrase from the act reads:

> [T]he continued regulation and taxation by the several states of the business of insurance is in the public interest, and that silence on the part of Congress shall not be construed to impose any barrier to the regulation or taxation of such business by the several states.[150]

As such, there are fifty different statutes relating to insurance regulation. Therefore, the captive must research and understand insurance regulation thoroughly in the state of proposed

---

147 *Id.*
148 For a general copy of a standard form, see the document located at the Maine Department of Insurance, www.maine.gov/pfr/**insurance/**forms/pdf/fsblty.pdf
149 1 Couch on Insurance Section 2:4.
150 *Id.*

incorporation. Because this may increase the cost of overall compliance, it must be part of the feasibility study.

Additionally, because of the fifty-state patchwork of insurance regulations, it is possible that a captive could inadvertently make legal contact with a jurisdiction, thereby becoming subject to that state's regulations and increasing overall compliance costs for the captive. In general, any activity directed at a prospect in a jurisdiction will allow that jurisdiction to claim regulatory jurisdiction.[151] However, the actual facts and circumstances of each particular event will determine whether a jurisdiction has the right to claim regulatory jurisdiction. Again, this highlights the importance of thoroughly researching any jurisdiction that the captive might come into contact with to determine whether that contact would increase compliance costs.

Once the domicile choice is made and the feasibility study is finished, the next step is to begin the formal steps for creating a captive insurer. The following discussion will take the longest path possible through the process of forming a captive; some jurisdictions will not use all of these steps.

### Steps to Form a Captive in US Jurisdictions

**Initial phone consultation**: several jurisdictions require an initial phone consultation with the commissioner. For example, Vermont requires a phone conference to discuss the

---

151 Brown, *Structuring and Operating a Captive*, 155, 165: "In deciding whether activity by an insurer constitutes 'doing an insurance business' courts have generally held that any activities directed to the forum state satisfy the test."

proposed captive,[152] as does South Carolina,[153] and Hawaii.[154] Before this meeting, the applicant must supply a synopsis of the captive's proposed business plan and the parent company's financial statements. The commissioner will review these documents for the two- to three-week period before the phone conversation. The purpose of this call is essentially to pre-screen the applicants, thereby preventing unwanted captives from entering the market. A state with this requirement mandates the captive perform a high level of due diligence before the meeting.

**Some states require two state-level approvals.** The first requires a finding that establishing the captive is in the best interest of the state.[155] To make this determination, the commissioner will consider:

(i) The character, reputation, financial standing and purposes of the incorporators;
(ii) The character, reputation, financial responsibility, insurance experience and business qualifications of the officers and directors; and

---

152 Vermont Department of Banking, Insurnace, Securities and Health Care Administration, Steps to Form a Captve, http://www.bishca.state.vt.us/captives/steps-form-captive

153 South Carolina Department of Insurance, Captives Formation and Licensing, http://doi.sc.gov/captives/Pages/FormationandLicensing.aspx .

154 Hawaii Department of Commerce and Consumer Affairs, Formation and Implementation Procedures, http://hawaii.gov/dcca/areas/captive/setting-up-a-captive.

155 See R.I. Gen. Laws Section 27-43-2(d): The captive must "promote the general good of the state"; see also Utah Code Ann. Section 31A-37-301(4)(a) ; Vt. Stat. Ann. Tit.8, section 6006(d)(1)(A) ; W. Va. Code Section 33-31-6(d)(1)(A).

(iii) Such other aspects as the commissioner shall deem advisable.[156]

The applicant must submit a detailed biography to comply with this requirement. The required information is detailed. For example, the Vermont biographical affidavit requires the applicant's full and maiden names, complete educational history (going back to high school), a ten-year residence history, a twenty-year employment history, the applicant's position with the captive, any professional/vocational licenses, a complete criminal history questionnaire, and any controlling interest in any insurance companies.[157] Finally, the affidavit must be notarized.[158]

**The applications for a captive insurance company that are submitted to the insurance commissioner are no less detailed.** For example, the Vermont application requires the names of the captive and the parent; the local agent; the captive's address; the location of the books and records; the original capital; the names and addresses of all the beneficial owners and their respective ownership in the captive; the names of the management firm, lawyer, claims handlers, actuary, and reinsurance broker (if applicable); coverage limits and reinsurance; a certified copy of the articles of incorporation; a feasibility study prepared by an actuary; a history, purpose, and size of association (if applicable); and a detailed plan of operation, which includes

---

156   W. Va. Code Section 33-31-6(d)(1)(A)(i)-(iii).
157   Vermont Department of Banking, Insurnace, Securities and Health Care Administration, General Licensing Forms and Instructions, http://www.bishca.state.vt.us/captives/general-licensing-forms-and-instructions
158   *Id.*

the risks insured, expected net annual premium income, rating program, reinsurance program, the organization and responsibility for loss prevention and safety, the loss experience for the last five years and projections for the next five years, and financial projections on an expected and worst case scenario.[159] In other words, the insurance commissioner wants a detailed plan of the company from the incorporators regarding the actual method of conducting business.

**Finally, there is the issue of original capital and surplus.** All states require the contribution of original capital. The amount and type of capital accepted (cash or letter of credit) will depend on the jurisdiction. In addition, all state commissioners have the legal ability to increase the amount of original capital based on the type and amount of insurance written by the captive.

Once all of this paperwork is submitted and reviewed by the insurance commissioner, the captive's application is either approved or denied. If approved, the captive can begin writing business.

### Running the Captive

A captive must be a stand-alone business for the IRS to recognize the deductibility of premiums paid to the captive.[160] One of the ways a captive can exhibit its stand-alone nature is through annual meetings as required by the corporation's bylaws. From

---

159 *Id*
160 *Harper*, 96 T.C. 45, 58. The third prong of the three-part *Harper* test is "whether the arrangement was for 'insurance' in its commonly accepted sense." Courts look to whether the insurance company was a fully functioning corporate entity to see if the company was in fact a legitimate insurance company.

an operational perspective, this means the bylaws must state where and when meetings are to be held, requirements for notice and waiver thereof, quorum requirements, voting rights and proxies, and whether telephone meetings are allowed.[161] Standard corporate practice requires these events to be transcribed and kept as official corporate records. It is imperative that the captive board members maintain rigorous adherence to the rules specifically outlined in the corporation's bylaws.

Captives usually use several different service providers.[162] For the board of directors, it is imperative to balance the business needs of the captive continually with the cost of using specific services. This monitoring of costs to run the captive should be done at regular intervals. For example, it should be part of the annual reporting process. It should also be done when the captive changes its business plan, when new members are brought in, when new board members are elected, when new lines of insurance are added or withdrawn, and when a member's or insured's corporate structure has undergone a change.[163]

Here is a list of services the captive will use.

**Domicile manager:** Most captive jurisdictions require a local manager or a manager approved by the insurance regulator.[164] The underlying policy reason for this is ease of communication; the insurance regulator needs to have a person within the jurisdiction to communicate with.[165] The domicile

---

161 Westover, *Captive Practices and Procedures*, 32.
162 Westover, *Captive Practices and Procedures*, 110.
163 *Id.*
164 *Id.*
165 *Id.* at 111.

manager has typically had the following duties: regulatory compliance, record retention, financial accounting, and cash and disbursements management.[166]

**Program management:** "The program manager is ... the catalyst for bringing the group together, and may also be a risk taker."[167] In other words, the program manager oversees the implementation of the overall insurance program, from risk reduction strategies to underwriting to servicing the policies.[168] It is his or her job to play quarterback for the captive program.

**Claims management:** The level of claims involvement will depend on the type of insurance the captive writes and the type of captive involved.[169] If the policy is fronted,[170] there may be

---

166  *Id.* at 111–12.
167  *Id.* at 11.
168  *Id.* at 113–14.
169  *Id.* at 115.
170  Captive.com, What's Up Front, a Guide to Fronting Arrangements, available at http://www.captive.com/newsstand/jlcovt/Fronting.html: "In its most common form, a commercial insurance company ('fronting company'), licensed in the state where a risk to be insured is located, issues its policy to the insured. That risk is then fully transferred from the fronting company to a captive insurance company through a reinsurance agreement, known as a fronting agreement. Thus, the insured obtains a policy issued on the paper of the commercial insurance company. However, economically, the risk of that coverage resides with the captive insurance company. There are several business reasons for this type of fronting arrangement—1.) The need for a licensed carrier to issue the insurance policy for particular risk. 2.) The need for a carrier with a minimum AM Best rating and/or the ability to meet other financial strength measures to issue the insurance policy for a particular risk. 3.) The potential ability to achieve tax deductibility of premiums by the insured through successful risk-shifting."

little need for a claims department.[171] However, a captive that writes many policies will have the need for a claims committee and an adjuster.[172]

**Legal counsel:** A captive will need the following legal services: litigation support (to defend claims), corporate secretarial (making sure the corporate paperwork such as meeting minutes is kept appropriately), regulatory advice (insuring the captive is operating according to the jurisdiction's code), and tax advice.[173]

**Audit:** Most jurisdictions require the annual report to be performed independently.[174] Audit firms can also help with accounting, regulatory compliance, and tax advice.[175] Regulators frown on "auditor shopping"—switching auditors in order to obtain a favorable opinion.[176] Usually, a jurisdiction will require a legitimate business reason when a captive changes auditors.[177]

**Actuarial services:** These fall into two categories, the first of which is rate development. The captive must review its rates periodically to ensure they are in line with loss experience.[178] The second category is "reserve reviews," where the actuary certifies the "adequacy of the captive's loss reserves."[179]

---

171   Westover, *Captive Practices and Procedures*, 115.
172   *Id.*
173   *Id.* at 116–17.
174   *Id.* at 117.
175   *Id.* at 117–18.
176   *Id.* at 118.
177   *Id.*
178   *Id.* at 118–19.
179   *Id.* at 119.

**Investment manager:** The investment manager oversees the management of the investment portfolio and may also give advice regarding basic captive issues.[180] Investment managers usually charge a fee, which is a percentage of assets under management.[181] As a result, it may not be advantageous for a small captive to utilize an investment manager, instead using the treasury department or treasurer of a member of the board of directors.[182]

Annual Reports

All captives in the United States are required to submit an annual report to the respective state insurance board. This report must usually be prepared by an independent CPA certified by the commissioner. The report must contain a statement of all the captive's assets, a statement of cash flows, a statement of liabilities and investments, underwriting expenses, reinsurance assumed and ceded, a statement of losses (both paid and unpaid), along with a complete list of all insurance claims paid during the year. In addition, the CPA must usually provide a report of the evaluation of internal controls,[183] a letter that outlines his or her own and the staff's experience,[184] along with a statement that he or she is indeed independent and that he or she understands his or her report will be filed with the commissioner.[185]

---

180   *Id.*
181   *Id.*
182   *Id.*
183   Ark. Reg. 073, section 4(C)(2).
184   Ark. Reg. 073, section 4(C)(3)(b).
185   Ark. Reg. 073, section 4(C)(3)(c).

## Shutting Down the Captive

In most states, one of the following seven reasons will allow a state regulator to shut down a captive:

1. Insolvency or impairment of capital and surplus.[186]
2. Refusal or failure to submit an annual report … or any other report or statement required by law or by lawful order of the director.[187]
3. Failure to comply with the provisions of its own articles of incorporation, bylaws or other organizational document.[188]
4. Failure to submit to an examination or any legal obligation related to the examination.[189]
5. Refusal or failure to pay the cost of an examination.[190]
6. Use of methods that, although not otherwise specifically prohibited by law, render its operation hazardous or its condition unsound with respect to the public or to its policyholders.[191]
7. Failure otherwise to comply with the captive statute.[192]

## Taxation

Subchapter L of the US income tax code differentiates between two types of insurance companies: life insurance and other

---

186 Ariz. Rev. Stat. Section 20-1098.09(1).
187 Ariz. Rev. Stat. Section 20-1098.09(2).
188 Ariz. Rev. Stat. Section 20-1098.09(3).
189 Ariz. Rev. Stat. Section 20-1098.09(4).
190 Ariz. Rev. Stat. Section 20-1098.09(5).
191 Ariz. Rev. Stat. Section 20-1098.09(6).
192 Ariz. Rev. Stat. Section 20-1098.09(7).

insurance companies.[193] The Treasury Regulations define a life insurance company thusly:

> An insurance company shall be taxed as a life insurance company if it is engaged in the business of issuing life insurance and annuity contracts (either separately or combined with health and accident insurance), or noncancellable contracts of health and accident insurance, and its life insurance reserves (as defined in section 801(b) and Sec. 1.801-4), plus unearned premiums, and unpaid losses (whether or not ascertained), on noncancellable life, health, or accident policies not included in life insurance reserves, comprise more than 50% of its total reserves.[194]

The code contains the same definition:

> For purposes of this subtitle, the term "life insurance company" means an insurance company which is engaged in the business of issuing life insurance and annuity contracts (either separately or combined with accident and health insurance), or noncancellable contracts of health and accident insurance, if—
>
> (1) its life insurance reserves (as defined in subsection (b)), plus
> (2) unearned premiums, and unpaid losses (whether or not ascertained), on noncancellable life,

---

193 Subchapter L, part I is titled "Life Insurance Companies"; subchapter L, part II is titled "Other Insurance Companies."
194 Treas. Reg. 1.801-3(b).

accident, or health policies not included in life insurance reserves,

comprise more than 50% of its total reserves (as defined in subsection (c)). For purposes of the preceding sentence, the term "insurance company" means any company more than half of the business of which during the taxable year is the issuing of insurance or annuity contracts or the reinsuring of risks underwritten by insurance companies.[195]

The service will look at the substance of the company's business to make the final determination regarding a company.[196]

## NON–LIFE INSURANCE COMPANIES

Code 26 U.S.C. 831(a) states, "Taxes computed as provided in section 11 shall be imposed for each taxable year on the taxable income of every insurance company other than a life insurance company."[197] Section 11 provides the following levels of taxation on non–life insurance companies:

(A) 15% of so much of the taxable income as does not exceed $50,000,

---

[195] 26 U.S.C. 816(a).
[196] Treas. Reg. 1.801-1(b)(2)" "Though its name, charter powers, and subjection to State insurance laws are significant in determining the business which a corporation is authorized and intends to carry on, the character of the business actually done in the taxable year determines whether it is taxable as an insurance company under the Code."
[197] 26 U.S.C. 831(a).

(B) 25% of so much of the taxable income as exceeds $50,000 but does not exceed $75,000,

(C) 34% of so much of the taxable income as exceeds $75,000 but does not exceed $10,000,000, and

(D) 35% of so much of the taxable income as exceeds $10,000,000.[198]

These rates are "compressed," meaning it takes a small amount of income ($75,001) to achieve a high (34 percent) tax rate. As a result, small companies should consider an 831(b) election. This allows a company that writes less than $1,200,000 of premiums per taxable year[199] to elect[200] to be taxed at the 26 U.S.C. 11(b) rates (see above) only on the company's taxable investment income.[201] Additionally, there is the 501(c)(15) insurance company, which allows for tax-free treatment of an insurance company that has less than $600,000 in receipts so long as 50 percent of the receipts are for premiums.[202] All premiums received by members of the affiliated group are counted toward this amount.[203]

---

198  26 U.S.C. 11(b).

199  26 U.S.C. 831(b)(2)(a)(i).

200  26 U.S.C. 831(b)(2)(A)(ii): "The election under clause (ii) shall apply to the taxable year for which made and for all subsequent taxable years for which the requirements of clause (i) are met. Such an election, once made, may be revoked only with the consent of the Secretary."

201  26 U.S.C. 831(b)(1): "In lieu of the tax otherwise applicable under subsection (a), there is hereby imposed for each taxable year on the income of every insurance company to which this subsection applies a tax computed by multiplying the taxable investment income of such company for such taxable year by the rates provided in section 11 (b)."

202  26 U.S.C. 501(c)(15)(a)(i)(I) and (II).

203  PLR 200809034, footnote 1 ("If an entity is part of a consolidated group, all net written premiums (or direct written premiums) of the members of the group are aggregated to determine whether

There are two points to consider under this election. First,

> For purposes of applying the Section 831(b) alternative tax, Section 831(b) applies a "more than 50%" ownership percentage to the definition of controlled groups under Section 1563(a), and attributes net written premiums received by all members of a controlled group to each taxpayer member.[204]

Second, if the company makes this election, then it "does not take underwriting income into account to determine its adjusted current earnings to compute its alternative minimum tax."[205]

Gross income for a non–life insurance company is the sum of the following:

(A) the combined gross amount earned during the taxable year, from investment income and from underwriting income as provided in this subsection, computed on the basis of the underwriting and investment exhibit of the annual statement approved by the National Association of Insurance Commissioners,

(B) gain during the taxable year from the sale or other disposition of property, and

---

the insurance company meets the requirements of I.R.C. section 501(c)(15)(A). I.R.C. 501(c)(15)(B). In this case, there are no other premiums to aggregate with the premiums ORG received during 20XX pursuant to I.R.C. 501(c)(15)(B).")

204 Mertens Law of Federal Income Taxation, *Taxation of Nonlife Insurance Companies*, revised by Ellie Grinols, JD, updated June 2009, Section 44:03.

205 Burstein, *Federal Income Taxation*, chapter 10, section x.

(C) all other items constituting gross income under subchapter B, except that, in the case of a mutual fire insurance company exclusively issuing perpetual policies, the amount of single deposit premiums paid to such company shall not be included in gross income,

(D) in the case of a mutual fire or flood insurance company whose principal business is the issuance of policies—
  (i) for which the premium deposits are the same (regardless of the length of the term for which the policies are written), and
  (ii) under which the unabsorbed portion of such premium deposits not required for losses, expenses, or establishment of reserves is returned or credited to the policyholder on cancellation or expiration of the policy,

an amount equal to 2% of the premiums earned on insurance contracts during the taxable year with respect to such policies after deduction of premium deposits returned or credited during the same taxable year; and

(E) in the case of a company that writes mortgage guaranty insurance, the amount required by subsection (e)(5) to be subtracted from the mortgage guaranty account.[206]

Insurance premiums[207] are the "amounts payable for insurance coverage."[208] These are gross premiums written less return

---

206  26 U.S.C. 832(b)(1)(A)-(E).
207  26 U.S.C. 832(b)(3): "The term "underwriting income" means the premiums earned on insurance contracts during the taxable year less losses incurred and expenses incurred."
208  Treas. Reg. 1.832-4(a)(4)(i).

premiums[209] and premiums paid for reinsurance."[210] Gross premiums include:

(A) Any additional premiums resulting from increases in risk exposure during the effective period of an insurance contract;
(B) Amounts subtracted from a premium stabilization reserve to pay for insurance coverage; and
(C) Consideration in respect of assuming insurance liabilities under insurance contracts not issued by the taxpayer (such as a payment or transfer of property in an assumption reinsurance transaction).[211]

Return premiums include amounts

(A) [w]hich were previously paid and become refundable due to policy cancellations or decreases in risk exposure during the effective period of an insurance contract;
(B) [w]hich reflect the unearned portion of unpaid premiums for an insurance contract that is canceled or for which there is a decrease in risk exposure during its effective period; or
(C) [w]hich are either previously paid and refundable or which reflect the unearned portion of unpaid premiums for an insurance contract, arising from the

---

209 Treas. Reg. 1.832-4(a)(6)(i): "An insurance company's liability for return premiums includes amounts previously included in an insurance company's gross premiums written, which are refundable to a policyholder or ceding company, provided that the amounts are fixed by the insurance contract and do not depend on the experience of the insurance company or the discretion of its management."
210 Treas. Reg. 1.832-4(a)(3).
211 Treas. Reg. 1.832-4(a)(4)(ii)(A)-(C).

redetermination of a premium due to correction of posting or other similar errors.[212]

Total premiums must also include 80 percent of the previous year's unearned premiums while also subtracting 80 percent of this year's unearned premiums.[213] The company includes the premium for the earlier of either the taxable year when the effective date[214] occurs or the year when the company receives "all or a portion of the gross premium for the insurance contract."[215]

---

212  Treas. Reg. 1.832-4(a)(6)(ii)(A)-(C).
213  26 U.S.C. Reg. 832(b)(4)9B0; Treas. Reg. 1.832-4(a)(3). See also Treas. Reg. 1.832-4(a)(8)(i): "The unearned premium for a contract, other than a contract described in section 816(b)(1)(B), generally is the portion of the gross premium written that is attributable to future insurance coverage during the effective period of the insurance contract. However, unearned premiums held by an insurance company with regard to the net value of risks reinsured with other solvent companies (whether or not authorized to conduct business under state law) are subtracted from the company's unearned premiums. Unearned premiums also do not include any additional liability established by the insurance company on its annual statement to cover premium deficiencies. Unearned premiums do not include an insurance company's estimate of its liability for amounts to be paid or credited to a customer with regard to the expired portion of a retrospectively rated contract (retro credits). An insurance company's estimate of additional amounts payable by its customers with regard to the expired portion of a retrospectively rated contract (retro debits) cannot be subtracted from unearned premiums." As Emanual Burstein notes, "The other 20% is not deductible because it is considered to be attributable to ... expenses insurers incur to generate their unearned premiums." Burstein, *Federal Income Taxation*, chapter 10, section e.
214  Treas. Reg. 1.832-4(a)(5)(i): "The effective date of the insurance contract is the date on which the insurance coverage provided by the contract commences."
215  *Id.*

The Treasury Regulations provide several important subtopics to the gross premiums written rules. First, when a company increases insurance premiums because of an increase in risk exposure, the company must include the increase in its gross premiums written in the "year in which the change in risk exposure occurs."[216] Second, when an insurance company receives a premium before the contract's effective date, the company may include the premium in "the taxable year in which the advance premium is written."[217] Third,

> If an insurance company issues or proportionally reinsures a cancellable accident and health insurance contract (other than a contract with an effective period that exceeds 12 months) for which the gross premium is payable in installments over the effective period of the contract, the company may report the installment premiums (rather than the total gross premium for the contract) in gross premiums written for the earlier of the taxable year in which the installment premiums are due under the terms of the contract or the year in which the installment premiums are received.[218]

Fourth, if the company issues a multi-year contract and the premiums can be paid "in installments over the effective period of the contract,"[219] the company can treat the contract as a "series of separate insurance contracts."[220] Finally, there is

---

216 Treas. Reg. 1.832-4(a)(5)(ii).
217 Treas. Reg. 1.832-4(a)(5)(iii).
218 Treas. Reg. 1.832-4(a)(5)(iv).
219 Treas. Reg. 1.832-4(a)(5)(v).
220 *Id.*

an important limitation on the amount of expenses a company can take regarding premiums written:

(A) The ratio obtained by dividing the sum of the company's deduction for premium acquisition expenses related to the insurance contract for the taxable year and previous taxable years by the total premium acquisition expenses attributable to the insurance contract does not exceed

(B) The ratio obtained by dividing the sum of the amounts included in gross premiums written with regard to the insurance contract for the taxable year and previous taxable years by the total gross premium written for the insurance contract.[221]

There are two methods of determining unearned premiums. If the risk of loss related to the unearned premium "does not vary significantly over the effective period of the contract,"[222] the company may use a pro rata method of allocation.[223] However, if the loss does vary significantly, the company may consider the "pattern and incidence"[224] of risk in determining the allocation of the unearned premium.[225]

Investment income for a non–life insurance company that does not make a small company election under 26 U.S.C. 832(b) is defined as

---

221 Treas. Reg. 1.832-4(a)(5)(vii)(A)–(B).
222 Treas. Reg. 1.832-4(a)(9).
223 *Id.*
224 *Id.*
225 *Id.*

the gross amount of income earned during the taxable year from interest, dividends, and rents, computed as follows: To all interest, dividends, and rents received during the taxable year, add interest, dividends, and rents due and accrued at the end of the taxable year, and deduct all interest, dividends, and rents due and accrued at the end of the preceding taxable year.[226]

Finally, a non–life insurance company includes gain from the sale or other disposition of property in its gross income.[227]

Losses are a different matter. Losses are "losses incurred during the taxable year on insurance contracts."[228]

Property and casualty insurers establish unpaid loss reserves when specified events occur that can result in an obligation to pay a claim (or claims) to or on behalf of an insured. Losses incurred include estimates of losses attributable to reported events as well as estimates of losses incurred that have not yet been reported (IBNR losses). Losses incurred also include estimates of losses for events for which liability has been contested by the taxpayer.[229]

An estimate of unpaid losses must be based on the most accurate estimate possible.[230] The company must be able to

---

226  26 U.S.C. 832(b)(2).
227  26 U.S.C. 832(b)(1)(B).
228  26 U.S.C. 832(b)(5)(A).
229  Burstein, *Federal Income Taxation*, chapter 10, section m.
230  Mertens Law of Federal Income Taxation, section 44:04.

establish "to the satisfaction of the district director"[231] that "losses incurred which represent unpaid losses at the close of the taxable year comprise only unpaid losses."[232] The taxpayer has the burden of proof in establishing whether the estimates of unpaid losses are fair and reasonable."[233] The director has the ability to alter the reported amounts, which "in [his or her opinion] are in excess of a fair and reasonable estimate."[234]

Losses are computed using a multi-step process:

(i) To losses paid during the taxable year, deduct salvage and reinsurance recovered during the taxable year.
(ii) To the result so obtained, add all unpaid losses on life insurance contracts plus all discounted unpaid losses (as defined in section 846) outstanding at the end of the taxable year and deduct all unpaid losses on life insurance contracts plus all discounted unpaid losses outstanding at the end of the preceding taxable year.
(iii) To the results so obtained, add estimated salvage and reinsurance recoverable as of the end of the preceding taxable year and deduct estimated salvage and reinsurance recoverable as of the end of the taxable year. The amount of estimated salvage recoverable shall be determined on a discounted basis in accordance with procedures established by the Secretary.[235]

---

231 Treas. Reg. 1.832-4(b).
232 *Id.*
233 Mertens Law of Federal Income Taxation, section 44:04.
234 *Id.*
235 26 U.S.C. 832(b)(5)(A)(i)–(iii).

Salvage value is simply the "proceeds from the sale of damaged property for which the insurer has taken title and/or recovering amounts from third parties who are responsible for the damage sustained by the insured (called subrogation)."[236] All insurers are required to use estimated salvage value in computing losses.[237] The salvage calculation includes all anticipated recoveries[238] based on "the facts of each case and the company's experience with similar cases."[239] The actual numbers used are based on the amounts the insurer includes in the annual statement submitted to state insurance regulators.[240] All salvage estimates must be discounted by one of two methods:

(1) By using the applicable discount factors published by the Commissioner for estimated salvage recoverable; or
(2) By using the loss payment pattern for a line of business as the salvage recovery pattern for that line of business and by using the applicable interest rate for calculating unpaid losses under section 846(c).[241]

"Discounted unpaid losses ... equal the discounted value of the expected stream of future loss payments."[242] They are computed in the following manner. First, the company uses the "unpaid losses shown on the annual statement filed by the taxpayer for the year ending with or within the taxable year of the

---

236 Burstein, *Federal Income Taxation*, chapter 10, section p.
237 Treas. Reg. 1.832-4(e).
238 Treas. Reg. 1.832-4(c).
239 *Id.*
240 Burstein, *Federal Income Taxation*, chapter 10, section p.
241 *Id.*
242 Burstein, *Federal Income Taxation*, chapter 10, section o.

taxpayer."[243] If the losses on the annual statement are already discounted,[244] and the discounting can be "determined on the basis of information disclosed on or with the annual statement, the amount of the unpaid losses shall be determined without regard to any reduction attributable to such discounting."[245] The company must discount "losses attributable to each accident year of each line of business."[246] Next, the company must use the "applicable interest rate,"[247] which is a rate "equal to the average of the applicable Federal mid-term rates effective as of the beginning of the calendar months in the test period."[248] Finally, the company must use either the loss payment pattern determined by the secretary[249] or elect to use its own loss payment history.[250] This election is made on the taxpayer's return for the year[251] and applies to the year of election and to each of the succeeding four years.[252] A company may not make an election for reinsurance on international business.[253]

All losses are lowered by 15 percent of the total of tax-exempt interest earned during the year,[254] the aggregate amount of 100

---

243  26 U.S.C. 846(b)(1).
244  26 U.S.C. 846(b)(2)(A).
245  26 U.S.C. 846(b)(2)(B).
246  Burstein, *Federal Income Taxation*, chapter 10, section o.
247  26 U.S.C. 846(a)(2)(B).
248  26 U.S.C. 846(c)(2)(A).
249  26 U.S.C. 846(d)(1): "Any loss payment pattern determined by the Secretary shall apply to the accident year ending with the determination year and to each of the 4 succeeding accident years."
250  26 U.S.C. 846(e).
251  26 U.S.C. 846(e)(2)(C).
252  26 U.S.C. 846(e)(2)(B).
253  26 U.S.C. 832(e)(3).
254  26 U.S.C. 832(b)(5)(B)(i).

percent[255] and non-100 percent dividends received deduction[256] and "the increase for the taxable year in policy cash values of life insurance policy and annuity and endowment contracts to which 26 USC 246(f) applies."[257] This does not apply to investments made before August 8, 1986, except for 100 percent dividends, which are handled thusly:

> the portion of any 100% dividend which is attributable to prorated amounts shall be treated as received with respect to stock acquired on the later of
>
> (I) the date the payor acquired the stock or obligation to which the prorated amounts are attributable, or
> (II) (II) the 1st day on which the payor and payee were members of the same affiliated group (as defined in section 243(b)(2)).[258]

Non–life insurers are allowed to deduct "all expenses shown on the annual statement approved by the National Association of Insurance Commissioners."[259] The company may deduct expenses incurred during the taxable year along with expenses "unpaid at the end of the taxable year."[260] However, all expenses are lowered by the total of expenses unpaid at the end of the preceding year.[261]

---

255  26 U.S.C. 832(b)(5)(B)(ii)(I).
256  26 U.S.C. 832(b)(5)(B)(ii)(II).
257  26 U.S.C. 832(b)(5)(B)(iii).
258  26 U.S.C. 832(b)(5)(C)(ii)(I)-(I).
259  26 U.S.C. 832(b)(6).
260  *Id.*
261  *Id.*

Non–life insurance companies are allowed the following deductions: standard business deductions,[262] interest,[263] taxes,[264] losses incurred from the payment and prospective payment of losses,[265] tax-free interest,[266] depreciation and depletion,[267] and charitable contributions.[268] The company may also deduct the following:

> Capital losses plus "losses from capital assets sold or exchanged in order to obtain funds to meet abnormal insurance losses and to provide for the payments of dividends and similar distributions to policyholders."[269]

> Dividends and similar distributions paid or declared to policyholders in their capacity as such.[270]

> Deductions authorized by subchapter B, part VI[271] and part VII.[272]

> Deductions authorized by subchapter D, part I.[273]

---

262   26 U.S.C. 832(c)(1).
263   26 U.S.C. 832(c)(2).
264   26 U.S.C. 832(c)(3).
265   26 U.S.C. 832(c)(4).
266   26 U.S.C. 832(c)(7).
267   26 U.S.C. 832(c)(8).
268   26 U.S.C. 832(c)(9).
269   26 U.S.C. 832(c)(5).
270   26 U.S.C. 832(c)(11). This does not apply to a mutual fire insurance company.
271   26 U.S.C. 832(c)(10).
272   26 U.S.C. 832(c)(12).
273   26 U.S.C. 832(c)(10).

"[D]ebts in the nature of agency balances and bills receivable which become worthless within the taxable year."[274]

"Nothing in this section shall permit the same item to be deducted more than once."[275]

**Small Insurance Company Election under 831(b)**

For a company that elects under 831(b) to be taxed only on its investment income, section 834 provides detail regarding the calculation of investment income. First, "'taxable investment income' means the gross investment income minus the deductions"[276] provided in section 834. Gross investment income has four components: interest, dividends, rents, and royalties;[277] any lease, mortgage, or other instrument from which the insurance company derives interest, rents, or royalties;[278] the alterations of any previously mentioned instruments;[279] and gains from the sale or exchange of a capital asset.[280] Also included in this total is "gross income during the taxable year from any (non-insurance) trade or business carried on by the insurance company."[281]

From the above total gross income, the company is allowed the following deductions:

---

274  26 U.S.C. 832(c)(6).
275  26 U.S.C. 832(d).
276  26 U.S.C. 834(a).
277  26 U.S.C. 834(b)(1)(A).
278  26 U.S.C. 834(b)(1)(B).
279  26 U.S.C. 834(b)(1)(C).
280  26 U.S.C. 834(b)(1)(D).
281  26 U.S.C. 834(b)(2).

1.) Section 103 tax-free interest[282] ("gross income does not include interest on any State or local bond"[283]).
2.) Investment expenses.[284]
3.) Taxes related to real estate owned by the insurance company. [285]
4.) Depreciation.[286]
5.) Interest paid or accrued.[287]
6.) Capital losses including both capital losses from the sale at a loss of a capital asset and "losses from capital assets sold or exchanged in order to obtain funds to meet abnormal insurance losses and to provide for the payment of dividends and similar distributions to policyholders."[288]

---

282  26 U.S.C. 834(c)(1).
283  26 U.S.C. 103(a); see also 28 U.S.C. 103(c)(1): "The term 'State or local bond' means an obligation of a State or political subdivision thereof."
284  26 U.S.C. 834(c)(1): "If any general expenses are in part assigned to or included in the investment expenses, the total deduction under this paragraph shall not exceed one fourth of 1% of the mean of the book value of the invested assets held at the beginning and end of the taxable year plus one-fourth of the amount by which taxable investment income (computed without any deduction for investment expenses allowed by this paragraph, for tax-free interest allowed by paragraph (1), or for dividends received allowed by paragraph (7)) exceeds 3 3/4% of the book value of the mean of the invested assets held at the beginning and end of the taxable year."
285  26 U.S.C. 834(c)(3). See also 28 U.S.C. 164(a): "Except as otherwise provided in this section, the following taxes shall be allowed as a deduction for the taxable year within which paid or accrued: (1) State and local, and foreign, real property taxes, (2) State and local personal property taxes."
286  26 U.S.C. 834(c)(4).
287  26 U.S.C. 834(c)(5). See generally 26 U.S.C. 163.
288  26 U.S.C. 834(c)(6).

7.) Special deductions allowed by part VIII of subchapter B (special deductions for corporations).[289]
8.) Trade or business deductions related to the insurance company's trade or business except that
   a. any item, to the extent attributable to the carrying on of the insurance business, shall not be taken into account, and
   b. the deduction for net operating losses provided in section 172 shall not be allowed.[290]

**Foreign Captives**

There are few tax benefits to incorporating a captive offshore. First, insurance income is specifically included in controlled foreign corporation income.[291] Second, while most CFC regulation is based on a 50 percent ownership rule,[292] inclusion in CFC income for related personal insurance income[293] is

---

289   26 U.S.C. 834(c)(7): "In applying section 246(b) (relating to limitation on aggregate amount of deductions for dividends received) for purposes of this paragraph, the reference in such section to 'taxable income' shall be treated as a reference to 'taxable investment income.'"
290   26 U.S.C. 834(c)(8)(A) and (B).
291   26 U.S.C. 952(a)(1): "For purposes of this subpart, the term 'subpart F income' means, in the case of any controlled foreign corporation, the sum of – (1) insurance income."
292   26 U.S.C. 957(a): "For purposes of this subpart, the term 'controlled foreign corporation' means any foreign corporation if more than 50% of – (1) the total combined voting power of all classes of stock of such corporation entitled to vote or (2) the total value of the stock of such corporation is owned (within the meaning of section 958(a)), or is considered as owned by applying the rules of ownership of section 958(b), by United States shareholders on any day during the taxable year of such foreign corporation."
293   26 U.S.C. 953(c)(1): "The term 'related person insurance income' means any insurance income (within the meaning of subsection (a))

based on a 25 percent ownership requirement.[294] This is a low threshold and is designed to bring association and risk retention group captive insurance companies' income into the US tax arena.

For the purpose of inclusion in CFC income, insurance income is defined as

> any income which
>
> (A) is attributable to the issuing (or reinsuring) of an insurance or annuity contract, and
> (B) would (subject to the modifications provided by subsection (b)) be taxed under subchapter L of this chapter if such income were the income of a domestic insurance company.[295]

This provision applies to all types of insurance policies—"property and casualty, liability, life, and health insurance, and, of course, annuity contracts of all kinds."[296] However, there is an exemption from inclusion in CFC income. First, the policy must be issued by a "qualifying insurance company,"[297]

---

attributable to a policy of insurance or reinsurance with respect to which the person (directly or indirectly) insured is a United States shareholder in the foreign corporation or a related person to such a shareholder."

294 26 U.S.C. 953(c): "(c) Special rule for certain captive insurance companies (1) In general, for purposes only of taking into account related person insurance income ... (B) the term 'controlled foreign corporation' has the meaning given to such term by section 957(a) determined by substituting '25% or more' for 'more than 50%.'"
295 26 U.S.C. 953(a)(1).
296 Reynolds, *Controlled Foreign Corporations*, chapter 5, section 515.
297 26 U.S.C. 953(e)(3).

which is a CFC regulated by its home country's[298] regulatory authority,[299] that is allowed to "sell insurance, reinsurance, or annuity contracts to unrelated buyers in the home country."[300] In addition, the company would be taxed as an insurance company if it were located in the United States[301] and it

> derives more than 50% of its aggregate net written premiums from the issuance or reinsurance by such controlled foreign corporation and each of its qualifying insurance company branches of contracts
>
> (i) covering applicable home country risks (as defined in paragraph (2)) of such corporation or branch, as the case may be, and
> (ii) with respect to which no policyholder, insured, annuitant, or beneficiary is a related person (as defined in section 954(d)(3)), except that in the case of a branch, such premiums shall only be taken into account to the extent such premiums are treated as earned by such branch in its home country for purposes of such country's tax laws.[302]

---

298  26 U.S.C. 953(e)(6): "The term 'home country' means, with respect to a controlled foreign corporation, the country in which such corporation is created or organized. (B) Qualified business unit The term 'home country' means, with respect to a qualified business unit (as defined in section 989(a)), the country in which the principal office of such unit is located and in which such unit is licensed, authorized, or regulated by the applicable insurance regulatory body to sell insurance, reinsurance, or annuity contracts to persons other than related persons (as defined in section 954(d)(3)) in such country."
299  26 U.S.C. 953(e)(3)(A).
300  Reynolds, *Controlled Foreign Corporations*, chapter 5, section 515.
301  26 U.S.C. 953(e)(3)(C).
302  26 U.S.C. 953(e)(3)(B).

In addition, the exempt contract must insure a risk in "a country other than the United States."[303] Finally, the company must derive at least 30 percent of its income from insuring "home country risks"[304] of "non-related people."[305] However, there are further complications:

> Superficially, this 30-percent test looks just like the 50-percent test that a qualifying insurance company must pass to get into the deferability game. There is a difference: the 50-percent test measures what percentage of a CFC's company-wide total ("aggregate") net written premiums is applicable home country risks. A CFC could pass this test without issuing any home country risk policies from its headquarters, by having all of its branches issue policies on home country risks (home, that is, to the branches). If the branches' home country policies were over half of the CFC's total net written premiums, the

---

303  26 U.S.C. 953(e)(2)(A).
304  26 U.S.C. 953(e)(2)(B)(i)(I).
305  26 U.S.C. 953(e)(2)(B)(i)(II). See also 26 U.S.C. 954(d)(3): "[A] person is a related person with respect to a controlled foreign corporation, if – (A) such person is an individual, corporation, partnership, trust, or estate which controls, or is controlled by, the controlled foreign corporation, or (B) such person is a corporation, partnership, trust, or estate which is controlled by the same person or persons which control the controlled foreign corporation. For purposes of the preceding sentence, control means, with respect to a corporation, the ownership, directly or indirectly, of stock possessing more than 50% of the total voting power of all classes of stock entitled to vote or of the total value of stock of such corporation. In the case of a partnership, trust, or estate, control means the ownership, directly or indirectly, of more than 50% (by value) of the beneficial interests in such partnership, trust, or estate. For purposes of this paragraph, rules similar to the rules of section 958 shall apply."

CFC would be a qualifying insurance company under the 50-percent test. The headquarters could have no exempt policies, however, since the 30-percent test for exempt contracts requires the issuing location (CFC or branch) to have at least 30 percent of its net written premium income attributable to home country risks. Code Sec. 953(e)(1)(C); Code Sec. 953(e)(2)(B)(i). Putting the two tests together, more than 50 percent of the whole company's premium income, and more than 30 percent of the income of each location, must be for home country risks in order to ensure that exempt contract income will result.[306]

Because of the lack of tax benefit from the CFC regime from captive insurance, most taxpayers opt to be treated as a domestic corporation. To qualify for the election, the corporation must be a CFC "by substituting '25% or more' for 'more than 50%'"[307] in the ownership requirement of a controlled foreign corporation.[308] Second, the company would be taxed under the US insurance tax section of the code "if it were a domestic corporation."[309] Third, the company must make an election that will apply to "all subsequent taxable years unless revoked

---

306 Reynolds, Controlled Foreign Corporations, Chapter 5, Section 515
307 26 U.S.C. 953(d)(1)(A).
308 26 U.S.C. 957(a): "For purposes of this subpart, the term 'controlled foreign corporation' means any foreign corporation if more than 50% of – (1) the total combined voting power of all classes of stock of such corporation entitled to vote, or (2) the total value of the stock of such corporation, is owned (within the meaning of section 958(a)), or is considered as owned by applying the rules of ownership of section 958(b), by United States shareholders on any day during the taxable year of such foreign corporation."
309 26 U.S.C. 953(d)(1)(B).

with the consent of the Secretary."[310] Regardless of whether the company makes an election to be taxed as a domestic company, it will compute its CFC income "as if the CFC were a domestic company."[311]

---

[310] 26 U.S.C. 953(d)(2)(A).
[311] Reynolds, *Controlled Foreign Corporations*, chapter 5, section 515.

# Part II: A Case Law History of Captive Insurance

## Introduction

### An Introduction to the History of US Captive Insurance Case Law

The IRS spent approximately forty years (roughly 1960–2000) aggressively fighting captive insurance companies. Additionally, the case law affecting the structure of captive insurance companies goes back to the early 1900s. As a result, there is a rich case law history that the practitioner must know in order to structure a captive insurance company in a manner that avoids an IRS challenge.

The purpose of this section is to present the case history in a comprehensive manner. The cases are presented in chronological order. Each section begins with an outline of the relevant facts, followed by an explanation of the court's reasoning. This will allow the practitioner to understand what particular structures have drawn IRS scrutiny along with how the courts have analyzed the law relative to captive insurers. I would strongly encourage anyone reading this section to also read the complete cases.

All of this legal fighting could have been avoided if a company could simply set aside money for a foreseen or unforeseen event. However, this is not possible under the law. Several companies tried this in the early 1900s. These are the "Reserve Cases" because in all of them, a company foresaw a contingency for which they set aside money.[312] All of the companies attempted to deduct the payments to the reserve fund, only to have the IRS challenge these payments as non-deductible. The courts ruled for the service based on two theories. The first was based on a strict reading of the code that did not specifically allow a deduction for payments to a reserve account.[313] The second argument—which is far more potent—is that allowing reserves would encourage earnings manipulation.[314] A contemporary example of this concern occurred in 2006 when Exxon earned a record amount of revenue. At the time, there were calls for a windfall profits tax on the company. If Exxon could set aside money in a reserve for this contingency and then deduct the payment to the fund, Exxon could manipulate its earnings. In the year of the deduction, it could lower its taxable income by claiming there was a possible contingency, and then when its taxable income was low, it could argue the contingency no longer existed and then bring the reserve back onto its balance sheet. The service and the courts wanted to prevent this type of earnings manipulation, so they disallowed this type of contingency planning.

One case from the late 1950s could have ended this problem as well. In *United States v. Weber*, the taxpayer and other

---

312 For example, see *Pan-American Hide*, 1 B.T.A. 1249.
313 *Pan-American Hide* (1 B.T.A. 1249) at 1250.
314 *Spring Canyon Coal v. C.I.R.*, 43 F.2d 78, 79 (10th Circuit).

companies owned property in the middle of a flood plane but because of recent loss experience could not obtain flood insurance on the open market.[315] The companies banded together to form an insurance cooperative.[316] The insurance cooperative was licensed by the state authorities.[317] Several participants obtained a private letter ruling regarding the viability of the transaction.[318] However, the IRS later challenged the transaction and lost. In response to the loss, the IRS issued a revenue ruling where it simply stated it would not follow the court's decision.[319] Had the IRS instead issued a ruling or series of rulings whereby it sanctioned certain structures required by business necessity (as the facts in this case clearly indicated and as the IRS later did with Revenue Rulings 2002-89, 2002-90, and 2002-91), thirty years of needless litigation could have been avoided.

After that decision, several facts led to the continual development of captive insurance. The most prominent was that certain business activities were either no longer insurable or only insurable at prohibitive rates. The companies in the cases that follow were involved in diverse industries, such as offshore oil development,[320]

---

315 *Weber Paper*, 320 F.2d 199, 201.
316 *Weber Paper*, 204 F.Supp.394, 395-96.
317 *Id*.
318 *Weber Paper*, 320 F.2d 199, 201-2.
319 Rev. Rul. 64-72: "Although certiorari was not applied for in the *Weber Paper Company* case, the decision will not be followed as a precedent in the disposition of similar cases, and the position of the service, as set forth in Revenue Ruling 60-275 will be maintained pending further judicial tests."
320 *Ocean*, 988 F.2d 1135.

international shipping,[321] hospital administration,[322] and aircraft manufacturing.[323] No one was attempting to devise an elaborate tax evasion scheme. Instead, all were attempting to solve a serious business problem—the need to procure and maintain an affordable insurance policy. In addition, despite the IRS's clear objection to captive insurance, private insurance providers and insurance service professionals continued to recommend, develop, and implement captive insurance as a viable business strategy.[324] This indicates that within the insurance industry, there was a strong belief in the eventual defeat of the IRS's position on captive insurance. This was followed by several states writing captive insurance statutes, which obviously attracted business.[325] In short, despite the IRS's objection, the insurance industry continued to act as though captive insurance was a viable business option for certain situations.

Not only were the legal winds blowing against the IRS, but so were the courts. The IRS's primary legal theory promulgated to thwart captive insurance was the "economic family" doctrine.[326] Under this theory, the parent company of a corporate group was so in control of the intra-corporate payments that any payment between companies was essentially moot.[327] The problem with this theory

---

321 See *Harper*, 96 T.C. 45, 47; see also United Parcel Service of America v. C.I.R., 254 F.3d 1014, 1016 (11th Cir. 2001).
322 *Humana*, 88 T.C. 197; and *Humana*, 881 F. 2d 247.
323 *Beech Aircraft*, 797 F.2d 920.
324 If there was a strong consensus in the legal community about the lack of captive viability, none of these structures would have been created.
325 Vermont Department of Banking, Insurance, Securities, and Health Care Administration, Data, Statistics and Links, available at http://www.bishca.state.vt.us/CapInsDiv/data_statistics_links.htm.
326 Rev. Rul. 77-316.
327 *Id.*

was if it were taken to its logical conclusion, all intra-corporate transfers would be suspect and could therefore be reclassified, essentially destroying the separate nature of corporations.[328] Later, the service would attempt to argue that a corporation was in fact a "nexus of contracts"[329] and then attempt an assignment of income argument,[330] but to no avail.

The service won the initial rounds of cases based on their use of the "economic family" doctrine and courts' acceptance of the service's arguments.[331] Essentially, the service argued the payment was not for insurance and therefore could not be

---

328   See *Humana*, 88 T.C. 197, 219: "More importantly, under the 'economic family' theory asserted by respondent, there seems to be no real distinction between disregarding transactions between related corporations and disregarding their separate status. However, I submit that, generally, transactions between ANY entities, related or unrelated, should be repudiated or recharacterized only if they are not legally or factually what they purport to be. The majority's reliance on financial reports to buttress its conclusion only fuels the 'economic family' fire; it consolidates two entities for tax purposes which are not permitted to file consolidated tax returns and, without a basis for so doing, erodes the long-standing principle of Moline Properties v. Commissioner, supra."

329   See *Kidde*, 40 Fed. Cl. 42, 55: "modern economic theory views a corporation as a nexus of contracts among individual stakeholders and evaluates corporate decisions based on how the individual stakeholders are affected. Consistent with this approach, Professor Niehaus argued that corporations do not bear risk but rather individual stakeholders bear risk. Hence, defendant argues, in determining whether risk shifting or risk distributing occurred herein, the court should focus on the individual shareholders of Kidde, and the risk faced by these shareholders is not affected when one subsidiary assumes legal responsibility for the claims against the other subsidiaries."

330   *United Parcel Service*, 254 F.3d 1014, 1016.

331   See Carnation Co. v. C.I.R., 71. T.C. 400; Cougherty Packing Co. v. C.I.R., 84 T.C. 948 (1985); *Beech Aircraft*, 1984 WL 988 at 1.

deducted.[332] In addition, the service relied on the "balance sheet" argument, which argues the following. The parent is the sole owner of the captive's stock.[333] When the captive makes payment on a claim, its stock price drops by the amount of the payment.[334] This in turn lowers the value of the parent's book value because the parent owns the captive's stock.[335] However, in the early cases, the companies did not present sophisticated legal defenses. The rulings state the companies were relying on the *Moline Properties* doctrine, whereby the court had to accept the separate nature of a company even if it was within the same corporate family.[336] The companies were arguing that the court was attempting to collapse the corporate affiliated group. The court overcame this objection by stating they were merely recasting the transaction.[337] However, this was often the end of the company's case as stated in the decision; there was no talk about the nature of the insurance company's business or the viability of the captive's financial structure, etc. In addition, the companies did not offer any strong experts who could testify that the parent and captive were in fact engaged in a legitimate insurance transaction.

---

332  *Id.*
333  *Id.*
334  *Id.*
335  *Id.*
336  See Moline Properties v. C.I.R., 319 U.S. 436, 438-39 (1943): "The doctrine of corporate entity fills a useful purpose in business life. Whether the purpose be to gain an advantage under the law of the state of incorporation or to avoid or to comply with the demands of creditors or to serve the creator's personal or undisclosed convenience, so long as that purpose is the equivalent of business activity or is followed by the carrying on of business by the corporation, the corporation remains a separate taxable entity."
337  *Id.*

That began to change with the *Humana* decision, where the court ruled that premiums paid from a subsidiary to a captive (which was also a subsidiary) were deductible because the subsidiary did not own any of the captive's stock.[338] Therefore, the subsidiary's balance sheet was not negatively impacted by a payment from the captive to the subsidiary. The deductibility of brother-sister premiums represented a landmark development in captive case law. This was followed by the *Harper* case,[339] where the court took a far more thorough and all-encompassing view of the parent-captive relationship. Instead of looking only at the stock ownership, the court now applied a three-prong test:

(1) whether the arrangement involves the existence of an "insurance risk";
(2) whether there was both risk shifting and risk distribution; and
(3) whether the arrangement was for "insurance" in its commonly accepted sense.[340]

This was a far more business friendly approach, as it analyzed the structure of the transaction between the insured and the insurer, the insurer's structure, and the diversity of the risks the insurer insured. In effect, the court wanted the captive to be a bona fide insurance company. So long as that was apparent—that is, risks were transferred from the insured to the insurer, and the insurer operated as an insurance company—the captive would pass muster.

---

338 *Humana*, 88 T.C. 197; and *Humana*, 881 F. 2d 247.
339 *Harper*, 96 T.C. 45, 47.
340 *Id.* at 58.

After about ten years of losses, the service finally gave up most of its legal challenges to captives. First, the service stated it would no longer use the "economic family" doctrine. Then it issued guidance about what type of structure would not be challenged. It issued Revenue Ruling 2002-89,[341] where it stated the captive must have at least 50 percent of its risks from a non-parent. In Revenue Ruling 2002-90, it stated that a parent that had at least twelve subsidiaries insured with the captive (with each subsidiary comprising no more than 15 percent of the captive's overall risk) would not be challenged.[342] This number was possibly lowered to seven in Revenue Ruling 2002-91.[343] Finally, the service issued Revenue Ruling 2005-40, where it stated it would write a private letter ruling regarding whether there was risk shifting between the parent and the captive, and whether the captive had adequate risk distribution.[344]

**The Non-Deductibility of Reserves**

Captive insurance would not have developed if a company could simply establish a reserve and deduct payments to that reserve. Unfortunately, several early cases—called the Reserve Cases—stand for the proposition that a company may not establish a reserve and then deduct payments made to that reserve.

In *Pan-American Hide*, the taxpayer set aside $275 in monthly payments to a reserve for fidelity insurance.[345] In essence, the

---

341 Rev. Rul. 2002-89.
342 Rev. Rul. 2002-90.
343 Rev. Rul. 2002-91.
344 Rev. Rul. 2002-45.
345 *Pan-American Hide,* 1 B.T.A. 1249.

taxpayer "assumed [the] fidelity insurance itself."[346] While the taxpayer attempted to argue this was similar to a depreciation deduction, the court stated depreciation and a reserve were two distinctly difference tax items.[347] The court's primary point was that a statutory discrimination existed between a deduction for depreciation and a reserve;[348] a strict reading of the code allowed a deduction for one (depreciation) and not the other (contributions to a reserve).

In *Spring Canyon Coal v. C.I.R.*, the petitioner "elected to become a self-insurer on July 1, 1919."[349] The company made this decision to comply with Utah law.[350] The company established a "Welfare and Compensation Fund" with two other companies and hired F. D. Brown to run the fund.[351] Mr. Brown kept each company's funds separate, issued a statement to each company "periodically," and set up an office from which he ran the fund.[352] The company kept the funds on its books as an asset for the entire time it had the fund.[353] Mr. Brown also paid claims from the fund to employees and collected a management fee.[354] The company deducted all contributions to the fund for the years 1920, 1921, and 1922.

The sole issue before the court was the deductibility of the company's contributions to its reserve fund. The court ruled

---

346 *Id.*
347 *Id.* at 1250.
348 *Id.*
349 *Spring Canyon Coal*, 43 F.2d 78.
350 *Id.* at 79.
351 *Id.*
352 *Id.*
353 *Id.*
354 *Id.*

against the petitioner, citing three reasons. The first was simply that the code did not allow a deduction for contributions for reserves as stated in *Pan-American Hide*.[355] The court observed: "The difference [between payment to an insurer and self-insurance] is one of fact; in the one case the expense of premiums is paid or incurred and in the other it is not. The discrimination, if such it be, is self-imposed."[356]

In other words, the court was using a strict reading of the deduction statute as it existed in 1930.

Second, the court noted the petitioner deducted the expense but then made a corresponding entry for the fund, which it also kept on the company's books.[357] While the court did not expand on this observation, the obvious conclusion is that the company did not transfer the risk outside of itself but instead moved funds among internal company-controlled accounts. In short, the company simply moved funds from different corporate "pockets" but kept the money on its books in one way or another.[358] The court observed that insurance involves risk shifting, which cannot happen when the taxpayer keeps the reserves in house.

Third, the court noted in recitation of the facts:

---

355 *Id.* at 80.
356 *Id.*
357 *Pan-American Hide*, 1 B.T.A. 1249, 1250.
358 *See Pan-American Hide*, 1 B.T.A. 1249, 1250: "The taxpayer's contention in effect is that it may take from its income in one pocket an amount equal to what it would have to pay as fidelity insurance premiums and puts this in another pocket and deducts it from gross income."

> It is argued that the petitioner has the right to treat payments into the fund as expenses, in that such accruals are available to pay its legal obligations. It is argued that the petitioner has the right to treat payments into the funds as expenses, and, in the event it later revoked the arrangement, to then charge itself as income with any balance repossessed; that is to say, the petitioner desires to select the taxable year into which this income shall be charged.[359]

This is a legitimate point. Any company that faces the possibility of an unseen contingency could set aside any amount of money it desired, claim it was a contingency fund, and then dissolve this fund when the "contingency" no longer existed. This is a situation that could be easily manipulated to a company's benefit and therefore should be prevented.

In *Appeal of William J. Ostheimer*, the appellant rented "furniture, carpets, rugs, chinaware, glassware, silverware and other articles and equipment"[360] for use in his restaurant. The lessee had to maintain the items in "as good condition as they are now and in such condition to be redelivered to the lessor at the expiration of the term."[361] To comply with that condition, the lessee established a reserve fund to which he contributed in 1918 and 1919.[362] The lessee deducted these contributions from gross income for the same years respectively. The commissioner disallowed these deductions and included them in the taxpayer's income.[363]

---

359 *Spring Canyon Coal* at 79.
360 Appeal of William J. Ostheimer, 1 B.T.A. 18, 19.
361 *Id.*
362 *Id.*
363 *Id.*

The court noted the taxpayer was an accrual method taxpayer.[364] As such, he would be able to make a deduction when a specific liability was actually incurred.[365] However, under the actual terms outlined in the lease, the taxpayer had not incurred a definite amount. The court noted,

> The liability to restore chattels as good as new or as good as when received when a lease is ultimately canceled or surrendered at some indefinite or indeterminate time in the future is not a present actual liability, and is not the actual incurring of an expense or liability.[366]

This is a central problem with any reserve. It is standard for the amount to be paid from the reserve to be unknown. This prevents the taxpayer from clearly establishing the amount of the actual deduction as the court noted.

A similar situation occurred in *Lucas v. American Code Co.*[367] In that case, the company was suing for "its failure to deduct from its 1919 gross income the amount for which judgment was recovered against it in 1922 on a contested liability for breach of contract in 1919."[368] In 1919, the taxpayer signed an eighteen-year contract with a salesman who was quickly discharged.[369] The salesman sued the company for breach of contract.[370] At this time, it was possible for a company to

---

364   *Id.* at 21.
365   *Id.*
366   *Id.*
367   Lucas v. American Code Co., 280 U.S. 445 (1930).
368   *Id.* at 447.
369   *Id.* at 447.
370   *Id.*

deduct a "loss occasioned by breach of contract ... in special situations."[371] The company asked the IRS if the company could deduct projected commissions that would have been paid to the discharged employee.[372] Although the IRS refused the request, the company established a reserve in 1919 and paid into it over several years.[373] The company made contributions to the reserve fund, and when the company settled the case from the reserve fund, it deducted the amount for the settlement on its 1919 tax returns and sought a refund.[374]

The court first noted "the income tax law is concerned only with realized losses, as with realized gains,"[375] which means the taxpayer must be able to identify a specific amount for tax purposes; a mere speculation will not do.[376] However, in 1919, the taxpayer was unable to provide a specific amount of the projected liability. At that time, "[t]he amount of the damages, if any, was wholly unpredictable."[377] As such, the amount of money set into the reserve "had no relation to the apprehended total loss."[378] Also of importance was the fact that the taxpayer used the accrual method of accounting, which required him to take a deduction "in the taxable year in which all the events have occurred that established the fact of the liability, the amount of the liability can be determined with

---

371 *Id.* at 450.
372 *Id.* at 447.
373 *Id.*
374 *Id.*
375 Id. at 449.
376 See the 8th edition of *Black's Law Dictionary* (2004): "The amount received by a taxpayer for the sale or exchange of an asset, such as cash, property, services received, or debts assumed by a buyer."
377 *Id.* at 451.
378 *Id.*

reasonable accuracy, and economic performance has occurred with respect to the liability."[379]

Because the taxpayer could not determine the amount of the liability, he could not comply with the above provision of accrual method accounting. In addition, the court agreed with a host of lower court decisions, which prevented a deduction for a reserve for a variety of reasons.[380] Therefore, the court denied the taxpayer the deduction.[381]

*Appeal of Consolidated Asphalt* dealt with the same issue for a cash method taxpayer.[382] The appellant was an asphalt company that had contracts with the City of New York.[383] The contracts stipulated the appellant would repair roads for a period of five years after completion of the contract.[384] To account for this contract provision, the appellant's accountant estimated that between 13 percent and 15 percent of the total amount received as payment on the contract would be expended on the repairs.[385] Therefore, the company set these particular amounts aside and deducted them from income for the years 1919 and 1920.[386] The commissioner disallowed these deductions and added them back to the appellant's gross income.[387]

---

[379] Treas. Reg. 1.446-1(c)(1)(ii).
[380] *Id.* at 452.
[381] *Id.*
[382] *Appeal of Consolidated Asphalt*, 1 B.T.A. 79.
[383] *Id.*
[384] *Id.* at 80.
[385] *Id.*
[386] *Id.*
[387] *Id.*

The court ruled against the company. In doing so, they focused on the company's cash method of accounting:

> The use of the cash basis means that net income must be determined by including all the gross income actually received and deducting only the amounts actually paid out. It would be an obvious distortion to return only the gross income actually received and deduct therefrom both the amounts paid out and the payments anticipated.[388]

In other words, the company cannot deduct an amount it thinks it might pay at some future date. As with the court in Lucas, the fact the taxpayer could not determine a specific amount was fatal; a taxpayer cannot deduct a mere contingency.

These cases disallowed self-insurance for the following reasons:

1.) The tax code allowed a deduction for business expenses, but not for amounts paid into an internally held reserve. This is supported by a strict reading of the statute.[389]
2.) Moving funds internally—from cash to a reserve or from one corporate "pocket" to another—does not shift the risk as required by insurance.

---

388   *Id.* at 82.
389   See also *Appeal of William J. Ostheimer,* 1 B.T.A. 18, 21: "The statute specifies what deductions are allowable and, except in the case of in insurance companies, no provision is made in the 1918 Act for the deduction of a reserve as such."

3.) The manipulation of gross income through the use of "reserves" and "contingency funds" was prevented as outlined in *Spring Canyon Coal*.[390]

4.) Both accrual and cash accounting methods require the taxpayer to deduct specific "realized" amounts. A taxpayer cannot deduct a speculative amount.[391]

Helvering

*Helvering* is a landmark decision in insurance law because it provides the basic legal definition of insurance: "Historically and commonly insurance involves risk shifting and risk distributing."[392] All future captive cases will use this definition and expand on it.

In *Helvering*, an eighty-year-old woman purchased an annuity and a life insurance contract.[393] She paid $4,179 for the annuity and $22,946 for the life insurance policy,[394] making her total payment $27,125. The annuity contract allowed her to receive $589.80 per year for life.[395] The life insurance contract paid

---

[390] See also *Appeal of Consolidated Asphalt*, 1 B.T.A. 79, 81: "When estimating the reserve to set aside for a construction contract, the appellant's accountant doubled the amount set aside for the years in question."

[391] See General Counsel Memorandum 35340, May 15, 1973: "However, because anticipated casualty losses are contingent in nature, it is a firmly established principle of tax accounting that even as accrual basis taxpayer may not deduct amounts it adds to a reserve for insuring its own risks."

[392] *Id.* at 539.

[393] Helvering v. LeGierse, 312 U.S. 531, 532 (1941).

[394] *Id.*

[395] *Id.*

$25,000 on her death.[396] From an actuarial perspective, the purchaser would have to live to eighty-four in order for her total payout to exceed her amount paid (and that assumes the insurance company does not invest the money received). She purchased these policies one month before her death.[397] The insurance company would not issue one policy without the other.[398] The proceeds of the life insurance policy went to her daughter, who did not include the amount of the life insurance proceeds in the estate tax return.[399] The commissioner disallowed the exclusion, and included the total amount of the insurance proceeds in the decedent's estate.[400]

To determine if the commissioner made the correct determination, the court had to define "insurance." The court first looked through the various insurance statutes before arriving at this definition: "We think the fair import of subsection [g] is that the amounts must be received as the result of a transaction which involved an actual 'insurance risk' at the time the transaction was executed. Historically and commonly insurance involves risk shifting and risk distributing."[401]

While the court did not provide a definition of "risk distribution," they did provide this definition of risk shifting: "Implicit in this provision is acknowledgement of the fact that usually insurance payable to specific beneficiaries is designed to shift to a group of individuals the risk of premature death

---

396 *Id.*
397 *Id.*
398 *Id.*
399 *Id.* at 537.
400 *Id.*
401 *Id.* at 539.

of the one upon whom the beneficiaries are dependent for support."[402] In other words, person X has a specific risk, here being death. When the insured dies, there is a risk that the persons who depend on person X will be impacted negatively. By purchasing life insurance, person X is shifting the risk of his loss away from the people who depend on him (who would be hurt when person X dies) and onto the insurance company (who will pay the beneficiaries a specific amount of money to compensate them for the risk of loss).

On the other hand, risk distribution is seen from the insurer's perspective. Essentially, the insurer must have a large enough pool of insured companies so that a claim by one company does not so negatively impact the insurance company as to make it bankrupt. As the court explained in *Harper*, "'risk distributing' means that the party assuming the risk distributes his potential liability, in part, among others."[403] Another way to describe the concept is the following:

> Risk distribution occurs when particular risks are combined in a pool with other, independently insured risks. By increasing the total number of independent, randomly occurring risks that a corporation faces (by placing risks in a larger pool), the corporation benefits from the mathematical concept of the law of large numbers in that the ratio of actual to expected losses tends to approach one.[404]

---

402  *Id.* at 540.
403  *Harper*, 96 T.C. 45, 58-59.
404  *Kidde*, 40 Fed. Cl. 42, 53.

In other words, insurance must exist from both sides of the issue—from the insured's and the insurer's perspective.[405] All of the case law regarding captive insurance will use the above definition of insurance.

Moline Properties

*Moline Properties* requires courts to recognize the separate legal existence of a corporation so long as the corporation is a legitimate business entity—that is, the corporation is not formed as a sham. This would become a bedrock issue in the post-Humana taxpayer victories.

In *Moline Properties*, Uly Thompson organized Moline Properties as a Florida corporation.[406] Thompson transferred a mortgaged property to the corporation in 1928.[407] A trustee who represented Thompson's creditors held the stock of the corporation as security for another of Thompson's loans.[408] The corporation sold the property in 1933.[409] The corporation reported a loss in 1934 and a profit in 1935 and 1936.[410] Thompson "filed a claim for refund on petitioner's behalf in 1934 and sought to report the 1935 gain as his individual return."[411] Thompson also reported the 1936 gain on his individual return.[412] In other words, the primary shareholder attempted to report corporate income as individual income.

---

405  Sears Roebuck v. C.I.R., 972 F.2d 858 (7th Cir. 1992).
406  *Moline Properties*, 319 U.S. 436 (1943).
407  *Id.*
408  *Id.*
409  *Id.*
410  *Id.* at 438.
411  *Id.*
412  *Id.*

The question is whether the corporation or Thompson is responsible for the taxes from the sale of property.[413] The court ruled thusly:

> The doctrine of corporate entity fills a useful purpose in business life. Whether the purpose be to gain an advantage under the law of the state of incorporation or to avoid or to comply with the demands of creditors or to serve the creator's personal or undisclosed convenience, so long as that purpose is the equivalent of business activity or is followed by the carrying on of business by the corporation, the corporation remains a separate taxable entity.[414]

In other words, the corporate form will be respected so long as it serves a legitimate business purpose.

This decision has an important impact on the idea of captive insurance and the IRS's desire to challenge the legal validity of a captive insurance company. Typically, a captive insurance company is a wholly owned subsidiary of a parent corporation. Under *Moline Properties*, a court must recognize the captive's separate corporate existence so long as the subsidiary is formed for a legitimate corporate purpose. As the IRS's general counsel noted,

> [t]o successfully defeat corporate identity, it must be shown that the corporation was formed solely for tax purposes and has no substantive business activity.

---

413  *Id.*
414  *Id.* at 438-39.

When the corporation is sufficiently capitalized and maintains the indicia of business operations, its corporate identity is rarely denied.[415]

Further complicating a possible legal challenge to captive insurance companies were two cases: *Consumers Oil Corporation of Trenton v. United States* and *United States v. Weber Paper Company*.

**The Flood Plane Cases**

The "Flood Plane" cases that follow are important for three reasons. First, they illustrate one of the primary reasons captive insurance continued to develop: business necessity. Businesses with certain types of risks could not obtain insurance at all or could only obtain insurance at unaffordable rates, thereby driving them to form their own insurance company. Second, the IRS lost the second Flood Plane case—*United States v. Weber*. Captive insurance litigation could have been avoided entirely if the service had merely accepted this decision. However, in response to this defeat, the IRS issued Revenue Ruling 64-72, stating,

> Although certiorari was not applied for in the *Weber Paper Company* case, the decision will not be followed as a precedent in the disposition of similar cases, and the position of the service, as set forth in Revenue Ruling 60-275, will be maintained pending further judicial tests.[416]

---

415  Gen. Couns. Mem. 35340, May 15, 1973.
416  Rev. Rul. 64-72.

This is the third reason the Flood Plane cases are important: the IRS refused to accept a court's decision, thereby setting up the next round of captive insurance litigation.

**Consumers Oil**

In *Consumers Oil*, the plaintiff leased a plant located on the bank of the Delaware River, which was subject to flooding problems.[417] The plaintiff could not obtain flood insurance on the property.[418] The plaintiff established a trust fund run by company directors to hold payments as insurance against flood damage.[419] The trust was revocable if the underlying business reason for establishing the trust was no longer valid or the plaintiff ceased doing business.[420] The company made two payments into the fund—$15,559.58 in 1955 and $17,817.84 in 1956—and deducted each as an "ordinary and necessary business expense" in the year of payment,[421] treating the payments as an insurance premium. No payments for flood damage were paid from the fund.[422] The commissioner disallowed these amounts paid, claiming they were not insurance deductions.

The court agreed with the service for two reasons. First, the amounts paid remained entirely under the control of the plaintiff and would be repaid to the plaintiff in the event the fund terminated.[423] This is analogous to the reasoning in

---

417 *Consumers Oil*, 188 F. Supp. 796, 797.
418 *Id.* at 798.
419 *Id.* at 797.
420 *Id.*
421 *Id.*
422 *Id.*
423 *Id.*

*Spring Canyon Coal* where the court was concerned about a company using reserves to manipulate earnings.[424] The court continued this line of reasoning first started in *Spring Canyon Coal* by stating this arrangement was nothing more than a voluntary segregation of funds.[425]

Second, in *Consumers Oil*, the plaintiff established a trust to receive "insurance" payments, hoping this would provide enough separation between the company and the funds. Remember: a primary problem in the reserve cases was that reserves simply moved funds among different corporate "pockets," but eventually, all the funds were kept under the same corporate umbrella.[426] However, the court did not agree with this tactic, ruling, "The mere fact that the transaction was cased in the form of a trust cannot avail the plaintiff."[427]

**Revenue Ruling 60-275**

The IRS expanded its position to similar arrangements and outlined them in Revenue Ruling 60-275 where a contract carrier (who transported cars from an auto assembly plant)

---

[424] *Spring Canyon Coal*, 43 F.2d 78, 79: "It is argued that the petitioner has the right to treat payments into the funds as expenses, and, in the event it later revoked the arrangement, then to charge itself as income with any balance repossessed; that is to say, the petitioner desires to select the taxable year into which this income shall be charged."
[425] *Consumers Oil*, 188 F. Supp. at 798.
[426] *See Pan-American Hide*, 1 B.T.A. 1249, 1250: "The taxpayer's contention in effect is that it may take from its income in one pocket an amount equal to what it would have to pay as fidelity insurance premiums and puts this in another pocket and deduct it from gross income."
[427] *Consumers Oil*, 188 F. Supp. at 798.

leased a facility next to a river.[428] To provide for flood insurance, the company established an "insurance exchange" with other companies that shared the same risk of possible flood damage.[429] Unlike the plaintiff in *Consumer's Oil*, here there are multiple parties contributing to the fund.[430] Each company paid a "premium," "the total of which deposits by each subscriber is not in excess of the total insurance coverage desired by the subscriber."[431] The "premium" was divided, with 1 percent going to a general fund and the remainder to a catastrophic loss account.[432] The funds were commingled for investment purposes and managed by a third party.[433] Any investment gains were paid into an "individual surplus account," which the recipient could apply to his annual premiums or withdraw.[434] Finally, different risks were subdivided into flood, location, and flood district, and the loss account was credited with "the pro rata share of the payments of the adjusted losses incurred by similarly classified subscribers."[435]

The service first noted that deposits into reserves are non-deductible.[436] Next, the service noted that under the legal definition of insurance,[437] there must be risk distribution.[438]

---

428 Rev. Rul. 60-275.
429 *Id.*
430 *Id.*
431 *Id.*
432 *Id.*
433 *Id.*
434 *Id.*
435 *Id.*
436 *Id.* See also *Pan-American Hide,* 1 B.T.A. 1249; *Spring Canyon Coal,* 43 F.2d 78.
437 See *Helvering,* 312 U.S. 531, 539: "Historically and commonly insurance involves risk shifting and risk distributing."
438 *Id.*

Because each subscriber was classified with other companies in the same geographic area, it was highly doubtful there would be any risk distribution.[439] For example, a flood in a specific area would impact all the companies in that area, and each company's respective payment would be deducted from the catastrophe loss account. The fund would be impacted severely as a result, thereby preventing true risk shifting.[440] In addition, the payment would essentially be a return of the taxpayer's deposit, once again making the fund more like a group of separate reserve accounts rather than insurance. However, the 1 percent allocated to the general fund is for a "fixed liability deductible as an actual insurance expense."[441]

Not dealt with in this revenue ruling is how to jibe its conclusions with the idea of mutual insurance—a situation where "several persons have joined together for their united protection, each member contributing to a fund for the payment of the losses and expenses."[442] The earnings of the company—over and above the payments of the losses, operating expenses, and reserves—are the property of the policyholders.[443] This revenue ruling seriously hinders the service in recognizing a mutual insurer.

---

439 *Id.*
440 See *Kidde*, 40 Fed. Cl. 42, 53: "Risk distribution occurs when particular risks are combined in a pool with other, independently insured risks. By increasing the total number of independent, randomly occurring risks that a corporation faces (by placing risks in a larger pool), the corporation benefits from the mathematical concept of the law of large numbers in that the ratio of actual to expected losses tends to approach one."
441 *Id.*
442 3 Couch on Insurance, Section 39:15.
443 AM Best, Glossary of Insurance Terms, Available At http://www.ambest.com/resource/glossary.html#M.

This fact pattern differed from *Consumer's Oil* in one important respect: *Consumer's Oil* involved a single company setting aside money into a reserve.

### *United States v. Weber*

Although distinguishable on a key point, Weber is an important case largely because of the service's post-decision reaction. In *United States v. Weber Paper Company*, the appellee rented a building subject to flooding.[444] To alleviate the problem of not being able to obtain insurance, the Kansas City Chamber of Commerce proposed a reciprocal or inter-insurance plan, which was organized under the laws of Missouri and Kansas and named National Flood Underwriters.[445] Both the states of Missouri and Kansas approved the application of the company to transact insurance business in their respective states.[446] Two plan participants obtained a taxpayer favorable private letter ruling from the IRS regarding the deductibility of payments to the fund.[447] Finally at the national level, a possible addition to the tax code under section 162 specifically authorizing that "amounts paid or accrued for premiums for insurance against losses arising from floods" was unnecessary because "the existing statute and the regulations issued thereunder appear to be sufficiently clear with respect to the deductibility of premiums paid for flood insurance."[448] The plan utilized several provisions from other mutual insurance contracts and organizations—essentially copying provisions

---

444   *Weber Paper*, 320 F.2d 199, 201.
445   *Id*.
446   *Weber Paper*, 204 F. Supp. 394, 395-96.
447   *Weber Paper*, 320 F.2d 199, 201-2.
448   *Id*. at 202.

and clauses already used in other jurisdictions.[449] Like the fund in *Consumers Oil Company,* the taxpayer's payment was divided into a general reserve fund (which received 1 percent of the paid-in amount) and a catastrophe loss account (which received the remainder).[450] Funds were commingled for investment purposes, and credit amounts in the catastrophe loss account could be withdrawn on sixty days' notice.[451]

A key point of *Weber* is that this case has multiple plan participants instead of a single company as in *Consumers Oil*. This situation is analogous to a modern-day risk retention group where all parties share the same risk, and they are all owners of the captive.

The trial court ruled for the taxpayer, and the appellate court affirmed the judgment. The appellate court conceded the government had a good point in arguing that the taxpayer did not lose control over 99 percent of the deposit/premium, because the taxpayer could request a return of the money with sixty days' notice.[452] This does look a great deal like a reserve fund, which the government successfully challenged in *Consumer's Oil Company*. However, the appellate court upheld the trial court's ruling, which states,

> 3. The conclusions contained in Rev.Rul. 60-275, C.B. 1960-2, p. 43, that the premiums paid by the taxpayer under this plan of reciprocal insurance are "amounts

---

449 *Weber Paper*, 204 F. Supp. 394, 396.
450 *Weber Paper.* 320 F.2d 199, 203.
451 *Id.*
452 *Id.* at 204.

set aside by a taxpayer as a reserve for self insurance," and that such a premium deposit "represents a nondeductible contingent deposit to the extent it is withdrawable by the taxpayers," are not consistent with the facts disclosed in the case at bar. This is because they are based on the erroneous or irrelevant assumptions that there could be no real sharing of the risks because the occurrence of a major flood "probably would affect all properties in a particular flood basin"; that each subscriber is substantially underinsured; and the non sequitur that any proceeds received by the taxpayer in the event of flood damage would, therefore, in effect, be a return of the taxpayer's own money. Such conclusions are also inapplicable to the case at bar since they ignore the fact that the deposits pass from the control of the taxpayer, and that no portion thereof can be withdrawn by the taxpayer during the policy year in which they are paid. Since the facts assumed in said ruling are inconsistent with the operation of the inter-insurance plan shown by the evidence in this case and the findings of fact contained herein, said Rev. Ruling 60-275 does not constitute a correct interpretation of the law applicable to this case and should not be followed herein.[453]

The court is making the following points:

1.) Because the fund is insuring the same risk in the same geographic area for the same types of companies, the service is arguing there is no risk distribution. If there

---
[453] *Weber Paper*, 204 F. Supp. 394, 399-400.

were a catastrophe, the lack of risk diversity means a single catastrophe would literally deplete the fund. The court disagrees, noting the service's conclusion is correct only if each insured property in the same area is damaged to the same degree and that each insured that makes a claim is underinsured.

2.) The court notes the fund is in fact a separate legal entity—the plan participants relinquish control of their premiums to the fund, and the premiums cannot be withdrawn in the year of contribution. In effect, the court is using the *Moline Properties* doctrine (that the court must recognize a separate company so long as it is not organized in a sham transaction or alterego) without directly citing the case.

This case turned on the concept of risk distribution. The IRS unsuccessfully argued that because the mutual company divided all the participants into similar classes that grouped risks together, there was no risk distribution. Here the judge disagreed with that point, although neither party provides any concrete numbers or facts backing up their arguments. The judge merely said there was risk distribution and left it at that. Later cases would establish bright line rules as to what percentage of an insurance company's business had to be from outside sources.

There are several facts that—although not stated—probably moved the court. The first was the inability of companies to obtain insurance. The companies were not looking to undercut an existing provider or find a tax loophole. Instead, they were looking to provide themselves with insurance that the market was not providing. An inability to find adequate insurance would leave wide swaths of land in the area undeveloped—a most unwelcome development for the locale. In addition, both Missouri and Kansas officials signed off on the company. The company acted as a full-fledged mutual insurer—a situation that the IRS had specifically said it would recognize for tax reasons in a previous general counsel's memorandum. Finally, two of the taxpayers obtained a private letter ruling specifically stating the program would not be challenged. Paradoxically, the appellate court stated the letters had no bearing on their opinion,[454] although that is difficult to believe considering their obvious evidentiary value.

As previously mentioned, *Weber*'s key distinction with *Consumer's Oil* was the number of participants in the plan. *Consumer's Oil* had one company owning a captive (via a trust), while *Weber* involved a limited number of companies using a single mutual insurance company. The service could have published a revenue ruling outlining these key facts allowing one (*Weber*) to go unchallenged while preventing another (*Consumer's Oil*) from going forward. Or the service could have simply let corporate counsel figure out the difference. Considering the obvious economic need of the situation in *Weber* and *Consumer's Oil*, this would have made a great deal of sense. Yet the service obviously viewed *Weber* as a threat. As such, the service published Revenue Ruling 64-72, which stated,

> Although certiorari was not applied for in the *Weber Paper Company* case, the decision will not be followed

---

454  *Weber Paper,* 320 F.2d 199, 205.

as a precedent in the disposition of similar cases, and the position of the service, as set forth in Revenue Ruling 60-275 will be maintained pending further judicial tests.[455]

Although *Consumers Oil* and *Weber* are clearly different because of the number of insureds, the service is obviously concerned about taxpayers obtaining the ability to use closely held insurance companies. As a result, the service issued the above-mentioned revenue ruling stating they would continue to challenge most situations regardless of existing precedent.

**Revenue Ruling 77-316 and the Service's Initial Victories**

Once the service decided they would not follow the ruling in *Weber Paper*, they had to develop a legal theory outlining their position. Several general council memos ensued,[456] all of which eventually found their way into Revenue Ruling 77-316. This revenue ruling outlined several common foreign captive scenarios and explained whether the IRS would allow a deduction for premiums paid to these captives. Just as importantly, it provided an outline of the service's primary argument against captive insurance arrangements: the "economic family" doctrine. The IRS would utilize the legal reasoning outlined in this revenue ruling in several important government victories, which are still good law. The practitioner must know these cases to avoid running afoul of these rulings.

---

455  Rev. Rul. 64-72.
456  See Gen. Coun. Mem. 35340, May 15, 1973; Gen Coun. Mem. 35629, January 17, 1974; Gen. Coun. Mem. 37040.

Revenue Ruling 77-316 states,

> In each situation described [in the revenue ruling], the insuring parent corporation and its domestic subsidiaries, and the wholly owned "insurance" subsidiary, though separate corporate entities, represent one economic family with the result that those who bear the ultimate economic burden of loss are the same persons who suffer the loss.[457]

The bedrock of the "economic family" concept is the argument that because "such amounts [paid for insurance from the parent to the captive] remain within the economic family and under the practical control of the respective parent, there has been no amount 'paid or incurred.'"[458] In other words, the parent corporation is in such control of all subsidiaries that the subsidiaries' separate corporate form is meaningless. The logical outcome of this argument is that no intra-corporate family transfers would be recognized because the parent was in such control of the corporate group that every transfer and transaction was suspect.[459] Perhaps this is a primary reason why the courts never accepted the "economic family" doctrine.

The "economic family" doctrine directly contradicts *Moline Properties*.[460] Instead of treating the captive as a legitimate

---

457 Rev. Rul. 77-316.
458 *Id.*
459 See *Sears Roebuck*, 972 F.2d 858, 861: "The "economic family" approach asserts that all transactions among members of a corporate group must be disregarded."
460 See *Humana*, 88 T.C. 197, 219: "More importantly, under the 'economic family' theory asserted by respondent, there seems to be no real distinction between disregarding transactions between

separate corporate entity, the "economic family" doctrine collapses an entire affiliated group into one company, essentially ignoring a legitimately established business entity.

Additionally, the service argued that they were simply "examin[ing] the transaction for its economic reality"[461]—in effect making a substance-over-form argument.[462] The problem is that they misapply this theory[463] and do not advance any specific anti-avoidance theories, although several are possible.[464]

---

    related corporations and disregarding their separate status. However, I submit that, generally, transactions between ANY entities, related or unrelated, should be repudiated or recharacterized only if they are not legally or factually what they purport to be. The majority's reliance on financial reports to buttress its conclusion only fuels the 'economic family' fire; it consolidates two entities for tax purposes which are not permitted to file consolidated tax returns and, without a basis for so doing, erodes the long-standing principle of Moline Properties v. Commissioner, supra."

461  Gen Coun. Mem. 35340, May 15, 1973.

462  See Gregory v. Helvering, 293 U.S. 465 (1935).

463  *Humana*, 881 F.2d 247: "The tax court misapplies the substance over form argument. The substance over form argument is not a broad legal doctrine designed to distinguish between legitimate and illegitimate transactions and employed at the discretion of the tax court whenever it believes that a taxpayer is taking advantage of the tax laws to produce a favorable tax result for the taxpayer ... The substance over form analysis, rather, is a distinct and limited exception to the general rule under *Moline Properties* that separate entities much be respected as such for tax purposes. The substance over form doctrine applies to disregard the separate corporate entity where 'Congress has evinced an intent to the contrary.'"

464  *See Humana*, 88 T.C. 197, 218: "First, one has only to thumb through any text or hornbook on corporate tax law to see the arsenal available to respondent in related corporation transactions. Yet this plethora of available tools, whether codified or judicially developed, apparently is inadequate for respondent in this area; so he asserts an 'economic family' theory which has ominous ramifications within and beyond the captive insurance area."

For example, there is no mention of the alter-ego doctrine, in which there is

> a corporation used by an individual in conducting personal business, the result being that a court may impose liability on the individual by piercing the corporate veil when fraud has been perpetrated on someone dealing with the corporation.[465]

This doctrine is more often used in the parent-subsidiary context, especially where a unified business exists and the subsidiary is undercapitalized.[466] This was a fairly typical situation with some captives,[467] yet the service made no use of this argument. In addition, the service could have also argued the step transaction applied to the captive transactions using either the mutual-interdependence test[468] or end results test.[469] Yet the service did not use either of these theories.

---

465 *Black's Law Dictionary.*
466 *Emanuel Law Outlines: Corporations* (Emanuel Publishing Corp, 2000), 40-41.
467 See *Carnation,* 71. T.C. 400: Captive originally capitalized with $120,000 with the ability to demand an additional $2.88 million.
468 Mertens Law of Federal Income Taxation, section 43:228: "The mutual-interdependence test finds that the step-transaction doctrine applies where individual transactions were so interdependent that the legal relationship created by one transaction would have been fruitless without a completion of the series. The relationship between the steps, rather than their 'end result,' is examined."
469 King Enterprises v. United States, 418 F. 2d 511 (Ct. Cl. 1969): "Purportedly, separate transactions will be amalgamated into a single transaction when it appears that they are really component parts of a single transaction intended from the outset to be taken for the purpose of reaching the ultimate result."

The first fact pattern outlined in Revenue Ruling 77-316 is entirely insular:

> During the taxable year domestic corporation X and its domestic subsidiaries entered into a contract for fire and other casualty insurance with S1, a newly organized wholly owned foreign "insurance" subsidiary of X. S1 was organized to insure properties and other casualty risks of X and its domestic subsidiaries. X and its domestic subsidiaries paid amounts as casualty insurance premiums directly to S1. Such amounts reflect commercial rates for the insurance involved. S1 has not accepted risks from parties other than X and its domestic subsidiaries.[470]

In other words, the captive only deals with other subs—it writes no policies outside the corporate family, nor does it obtain any reinsurance. The captive is expected to stand on its own. Several cases successfully prosecuted by the IRS illustrate how the service attacked this fact pattern.

The plaintiff in *Stearns Rogers* designed and manufactured "large mining, petroleum and power generation plants."[471] In order to bid on projects, the company had to obtain insurance for its own contractors as well as its clients.[472] Starting in the early 1970s, the company "found it difficult or impossible to obtain from traditional companies the types and huge amounts of

---

[470] Rev. Rul. 77-316.
[471] Stearns-Rogers Corp., Inc. v. United States, 577 F. Supp. 833, 834 (Colorado 1984).
[472] *Id.*

coverage needed."[473] Therefore, the company formed a captive insurance company under the Colorado Captive Insurance Company Act.[474] In order to gain approval from the Colorado Insurance Commissioner, Stearns Rogers had to demonstrate the company could not find other insurance.[475] The plaintiff named the company Glendale Insurance Company, which only issued insurance policies for the plaintiff, the plaintiff's subsidiaries, and the plaintiff's clients.[476] Glendale did not use reinsurance. The plaintiff agreed to indemnify the captive for up to three million dollars. The plaintiff deducted payments it made to Glendale under the theory that the payments were insurance premiums.[477] The service disallowed the deductions,[478] claiming the payments were in fact self-insurance or payments to a reserve, which are not deductible.[479]

At trial, the service advanced its "economic family" argument,[480] while the plaintiff argued the payments were insurance premiums paid between two distinct corporate entities, thereby invoking *Moline Properties*.[481] After an analysis that determined the captive was formed for a legitimate business purpose (and therefore not a sham for tax purposes), the court ruled Stearns Rogers and Glendale Insurance were two distinct corporate entities that should be recognized.[482] Next, the court

---

473 *Id.*
474 *Id.*
475 *Id.*
476 *Id.*
477 *Id.* at 834-35.
478 *Id.* at 835.
479 *Id.*
480 *Id.*
481 *Id.* at 835-36.
482 *Id.* at 836.

explained the "economic family" doctrine of Revenue Ruling 77-316, citing *Carnation v. Commissioner*.[483] "The essence of that ruling [*Carnation*] is that there can be no deduction where, in actuality, there has been no shifting of risk outside the economic family."[484] To bolster its argument, the court distinguishes Stearns Rogers from *Weber Paper Company*, stating,

> Its [Stearns Rogers] problem is that in contrast with the Weber Paper Company, it did not ally itself with others similarly situated so that the risk of any one member's flood loss would be shifted to the "economic families" of the other insured members.[485]

In effect, because Glendale did not insure any other company's risks, there was no risk shifting. There was no insurance, because "profits and losses stay within the Stearns Rogers 'economic family.' In substance, the arrangement shifts no more risk from Stearns Rogers than if Stearns Rogers self-insured."[486]

The appeals court affirmed the district court.[487] They first noted that self-insurance plans do not constitute insurance.[488] They next noted that risk did not leave the "parent company." The payments for coverage went from parent to subsidiary, but the ultimate burden for losses was always on the parent."[489]

---

483   *Carnation*, 640 F.2d 1010.
484   *Stearns-Rogers*, 774 F.2d 414 at 837.
485   *Id.* at 838.
486   *Id.*
487   *Stearns-Rogers*, 774 F.2d 414.
488   *Id.* at 415.
489   *Id.*

In effect, the court is arguing Stearns Rogers established a reserve fund without actually stating the same. In addition, the appeals court sidesteps the problems of not properly applying *Moline Properties* to the fact pattern by noting,

> The separation [between the companies] is not ignored. Instead the focus must be on the nature and consequences of the payments by the parent and the Supreme Court's requirement that there must be a shift of risk to have insurance ... The comparison of the arrangement here made to self-insurance cannot be ignored.[490]

This is the exact same reasoning offered by the service regarding the possible problems of *Moline Properties*:

> However, we are of the view that the concept of independent corporate identity is not being challenged by the rationale espoused. We do not propose to ignore the taxpayer's separate identity. Rather, the proposed ruling examines the transaction for its economic reality.[491]

The service is making an anti-abuse argument by asking the court to look beyond legally and legitimately established corporate forms to see an "economic family." In effect, the service is advancing a new anti-avoidance theory.

---

490   *Id.* at 416.
491   *Gen. Coun. Memo.* 35349. May 15, 1973.

In *Beech Aircraft v. United States*, the plaintiff lost a jury verdict of $21,700,000 in 1971.[492] The old insurance policy did not allow Beech to investigate claims against the company or participate meaningfully in their legal defense.[493] As a result, Beech formed a captive insurance company in Bermuda on March 2, 1972, named Travel Air Insurance Company, Ltd.[494] Travel Air was originally capitalized with $120,000.[495] Beech paid a $1.5 million premium to Travel Air for a $2 million policy for the fiscal year September 1, 1971, to August 31, 1972.[496] Beech made no assurances to Travel Air that Beech would "pay any losses which occurred greater than the excess insurance carried by Travel Air, nor did it agree to further enlarge the capital structure of Travel Air in any event."[497] Beech obtained an additional policy from Fairfax Underwriters for $10 million.[498] While Travel Air sought outside business after 1973, that occurred after the period in question for this case.

The court's reasoning was short. First, they noted that a transaction's substance governs the tax consequences[499]— which is essentially an anti-avoidance argument. The court's primary ruling dealt with the corporate inter-relationship of Beech and Travel Air; because Beech owned a majority of Travel Air's stock, a payment from Travel Air would lower Beech's net worth: "Here the gain or loss enjoyed or suffered

---

492 *Beech Aircraft*, 1984 WL 988 at 1.
493 *Id.*
494 *Id.*
495 *Id.*
496 *Id.*
497 *Id.* at 2.
498 Id.
499 *Gregory v. Helvering.*

by Travel Air is reflected directly on the net worth of the parent Beech."[500] In addition, because Travel Air had a capitalization of $150,000, they would have to ask Beech for additional capital in the event of a payout larger than $150,000.[501]

Not stated, but certainly implied by the ruling, is the circular nature of the cash flows. Beech paid a premium to Travel Air, who would in turn pay Beech in the event of a claim against Beech. In effect, Travel Air was a reserve fund for Beech that simply stored funds until requested by Beech. Hence, the court's quoting of the primary anti-avoidance concept of substance over form in conjunction with this concern: "It is conceivable, though unlikely, that if no losses were encountered, the deduction of purported insurance premiums could become a tax loophole for the parent company."[502]

Situation 2 of Revenue Ruling 77-316 is the same as situation 1, except that the parent and subsidiaries pay premiums to a non-affiliated third party who reinsures 95 percent of the risk with a captive insurance company.[503] General Counsel Memorandum 35629 fleshes out the service's thinking regarding situation 2—although it is not given a formal name.[504] The service argues the taxpayer should be allowed to deduct any payment not reinsured through the taxpayer's captive.[505] In other words, risks that are outside the "economic family" and that

---

500  *Id.* at CONCLUSIONS OF LAW paragraph 4.
501  *Id.* at paragraph 5.
502  *Id.* at ADDITIONAL SPECIFIC FINDINGS OF FACT paragraph 14.
503  *Id.*
504  Gen. Coun. Mem. 35629, January 17, 1974.
505  *Id.*

follow proper insurance protocol are deductible, whereas any payments—either directly or indirectly—to an insurance company that is a member of the same corporate family are not allowed.[506] The service believes that in situation 2, the taxpayer is attempting to "authenticate its so-called insurance premium payment by introducing an independent insurer between it and its subsidiaries ... The whole transaction was carefully orchestrated to produce a single result – eventual placement of the insurance with [the captive]."[507] Again, the IRS is arguing this is essentially a sham transaction yet does not invoke any specific anti-avoidance doctrine.

The petitioner in *Carnation* was a food company that also made its own cans.[508] As a result, the company had workers' compensation insurance claims.[509] Carnation's board of directors resolved to "organize an insurance company in Bermuda to carry on the business of insurance and reinsurance of various multiple line risks, including those of petitioner and its subsidiaries."[510] As a result, Three Flowers Assurance Co. was formed on August 26, 1971.[511] Carnation purchased 120,000 shares of Three Flowers stock for one dollar per share.[512] In addition, the two companies signed an agreement whereby either could demand that Carnation purchase an additional 288,000 shares of Three Flowers preferred stock at ten dollars per share.[513] Next, Carnation applied for and

---

506 *Id.*
507 *Id.*
508 *Carnation*, 71 T.C. 400, 401.
509 *Id.*
510 *Id.* at 402.
511 *Id.*
512 *Id.*
513 *Id.*

received an insurance policy from American Home Assurance (a division of AIG), whereby American Home would insure up to $500,000 of loss from any one event.[514] This policy with American Home had a $100,000 deductible.[515] On the same day that Carnation purchased the insurance policy from American Home, American Home purchased a reinsurance policy from Three Flowers, whereby Three Flowers would reinsure 90 percent of the liability of American Homes from the Carnation policy.[516] American Home also agreed to cede 90 percent of the premium it received from Carnation to Three Flowers.[517] American Home would not sign the contract unless Carnation somehow provided assurances that Three Flowers was financially capable of paying on its policies.[518] To assuage this concern, Carnation represented that "it would provide for the capitalization of Three Flowers up to $3 million."[519]

The service made four arguments against this arrangement. First, under the arrangement, there was no risk shifting as required by law.[520] Second, the plan was nothing more than a reserve whose contributions were disallowed as deductions under law.[521] Third, the 90 percent payment ceded to Three Flowers remained within the same economic family and was therefore not "paid or incurred."[522] Fourth, in order for

---

514   *Id.*
515   *Id.*
516   *Id.*
517   *Id.*
518   *Id.* at 404.
519   *Id.*
520   *Id.* at 405.
521   Id. See also *Spring Canyon Coal*, 43 F.2d 78; and *Pan-American Hide*, 1 B.T.A. 1249.
522   *Carnation*, 71 T.C. at 405.

a deduction to occur, the payor must receive something of value. Because the petitioner ultimately bore the risk of loss, he received nothing of value and therefore could not take a legitimate deduction under 26 U.S.C. 162.[523]

Carnation responded by noting the service's arguments were premised on Carnation and Three Flowers not being separate entities.[524] Carnation then noted *Moline Properties* prevents this conclusion.[525] In addition, the two companies filed separate tax returns, indicating that for tax purposes, Three Flowers was not part of a Carnation consolidated group.[526]

The court based its analysis on the method established in *Helvering v. LeGierse*.[527] The court noted the insurance contracts in that case were interrelated; therefore, the court should analyze the facts in Carnation in a similar manner.[528] Additionally, the court noted the insurance contract between Carnation and American Home and American Home and Three Flowers were also interrelated and should be analyzed together.[529] This blunted Carnation's argument for the court to consider the companies as separate and distinct companies.

In ruling against Carnation, the court relied on the circular nature of the cash flows within this deal:

---

523 *Id.* at 405-406.
524 *Id.* at 406.
525 *Id.*
526 *Id.*
527 *Id.* at 407-408.
528 *Id.* at 408.
529 *Id.*

In the event of a covered casualty, the loss suffered by Carnation ultimately would be borne 90% by Three Flowers and 10% by American Home. The agreement to purchase additional shares of Three Flowers by Carnation bound Carnation to an investment risk that was directly tied to the loss payment fortunes of Three Flowers, which in turn were wholly contingent upon the amount of property loss suffered by Carnation. The agreement by Three Flowers to "reinsure" Carnation's risks and the agreement by Carnation to capitalize Three Flowers up to $3 million on demand counteracted each other. Taken together, these two agreements are void of insurance risk. As was stated by the court in LeGierse, "in this combination the one neutralizes the risk customarily inherent in the other."[530]

In short, the combination of the undercapitalization of Three Flowers's and Carnation's agreement to provide additional capital to Three Flowers was this structure's Achilles' heel. Three Flowers only reinsured risks from Carnation. Were Carnation to have several claims totaling more than $120,000 (Three Flowers original capital from its sale of stock to Carnation), Carnation would have to provide additional capital to Three Flowers. However, Carnation was the company making the claim that was depleting Three Flowers's capital. In short, a claim or combination of claims over $120,000 would force Carnation to pay itself, making this deal a pure example of self-insurance. The court did rule that the 10 percent of the risk that stayed with American Home was an insurance risk

---

530   *Id.* at 409.

and was therefore deductible.[531] This was in line with Revenue Ruling 77-316.[532]

*Clougherty Packing Co.* involved a different company but remarkably similar facts.[533] Clougherty was a California company that had an Arizona subsidiary, which in turn owned an insurance company named Lombardy.[534] Because Clougherty was involved in slaughterhouse operations, they had numerous workers' compensation claims.[535] Under California law, they were required to obtain insurance to cover these claims.[536] In 1976, Clougherty's insurance broker submitted a proposal to Clougherty regarding the formation of a captive insurance company.[537] Clougherty's management agreed, although they believed the captive should reinsure risks rather than provide direct insurance.[538] The company believed a captive would lower their workers' compensation costs.[539] Clougherty formed Lombardy insurance on July 22, 1977, and capitalized Lombardy with $1 million.[540] Later that year, Clougherty agreed to a reinsurance plan with Freement Indemnity, which called for Freement to provide the primary insurance policy to Clougherty, while Lombardy provided the first $100,000 of reinsurance to Freemont.[541] Under the

---

531 *Id.*
532 Rev. Rul. 77-316.
533 *Clougherty*, 84 T.C. 948.
534 *Id.* at 949.
535 *Id.*
536 *Id.*
537 *Id.* at 951.
538 *Id.*
539 *Id.*
540 *Id.*
541 *Id.* at 952.

plan, Clougherty would pay Freemont, who in turn would remit 92 percent of the premiums to Lombardy.[542] Clougherty made no promises or guarantees regarding future payments to its captive Lombardy.[543] Clougherty deducted $840,000 in 1978 and $1,457,500 in 1979 as insurance premiums.[544] The service disallowed the portion of the premiums remitted to Lombardy.[545]

In ruling against Clougherty, the court based its decision on several factors. First, they noted that "the operative facts in the instant case are indistinguishable from the facts in Carnation."[546] As such, the court made its decision regarding Clougherty from "within the parameters of Carnation."[547] The court first noted that three separate courts[548] had used the rationale of *Carnation* with no criticism—essentially validating the court's overall legal reasoning in *Carnation*. The petitioner tried to distinguish the facts in *Clougherty* by noting that the captive in *Clougherty* was adequately capitalized and did not have an agreement for an infusion of capital from the parent.[549] The court responded that the "financial viability of the captive is not controlling. The test continues to be whether the risk of

---

542  *Id.* at 953.
543  *Id.*
544  *Id.* at 954.
545  *Id.*
546  *Id.* at 956.
547  *Id.*
548  *Stearns-Rogers*, 577 F. Supp. 833; *Beech Aircraft*, 54 AFTR 2d 84-6173; Crawford Fitting Co. v. United States, 606 F. Supp. 136 (N.D. Ohio 1985).
549  Id. In *Carnation*, the petitioner initially capitalized its captive with $120,000. In addition, a contract existed between the parent and the captive that either could demand the parent to purchase an additional $2.8 million in preferred stock.

loss was shifted away from the taxpayer who seeks to deduct insurance premiums."[550] To that end, the court noted,

> When petitioner sustains losses covered by its workers' compensation insurance, 92% is sustained by Lombardy. Accordingly, because petitioner, through its wholly owned Arizona corporation, owns all of Lombardy, it has not shifted the risk of sustaining such losses to unrelated parties in exchange for insurance premiums, because the premiums were paid to the wholly owned subsidiary of its wholly owned subsidiary.[551]

The court's reasoning is that the payment from the captive will deplete the company's cash account, which in turn will lower the captive's stock value. Because the parent company owns all the captive's stock, the parent's balance sheet would decrease in value in proportion to the cash payment from the captive.

There are several other important points from the decision. First, the court expressly stated it would not use the term "economic family."[552] This is an important point, as an acceptance of this concept would have cemented the IRS's anti-captive argument into case law. In addition, the court noted they were not disregarding the separate corporate nature of the parent and captive. Instead, they were recasting the nature of the transaction:

> There are numerous situations in the tax law, both statutory and case law, where the separate nature of

---

550   *Clougherty,* at 957.
551   *Id.* at 958-59.
552   *Id.* at 959.

the entity is not disregarded, but the transaction, as cast between the related parties, is reclassified to represent something else, e.g. reasonable compensation or dividend, loans or contributions to capital, loans or dividends, deposits or payments, or other recharacterization such as permitted under section 482, Internal Revenue Code of 1954, as amended. We have done nothing more in *Carnation* and here than to reclassify, as nondeductible, portions of the payments which the taxpayers deducted as insurance premiums but which were received by the taxpayer's captive insurance subsidiaries.[553]

In effect, the court, in its ruling, is recognizing the separate nature of the companies. However, the court must recast the transaction (which it has the statutory authority to do), because there is no risk shifting and therefore no insurance.

The dissent makes great hay of the majority's arguments. First, it notes, "[T]he new theory would disallow a deduction solely because of the ownership relationship between an insured and insurer."[554] This is a solid point. The majority has now prevented any company from owning an insurance company and then purchasing insurance from that subsidiary. Next, the dissent notes, "There is no explanation as to the reason or principle that automatically precludes insurance between related entities."[555]

This is a natural by-product of the *Carnation* decision—a company cannot own an insurance company and then

---

553   *Id.* at 960.
554   *Id.* at 966.
555   *Id.* at 967.

purchase an insurance policy from that company, even if the policy conforms to industry standards and is issued at market rates. The majority has simply made it impossible for that to happen. Finally, "[t]he majority has stated, but not explained, how it is able to disregard the transaction in this case without crashing head-on into the holding of Moline Properties."[556]

This is the key problem of the majority's opinion. While the insurance company in *Carnation* was inadequately capitalized, leading to an adverse decision, Clougherty's captive had $1 million in reserves[557] and no agreement to receive additional funds from the parent. Nothing in the case indicates the insurance policies issued by the captive were outside the industry norm. In addition, there is no indication that the company was in any way attempting to evade taxation. In fact, the company could lower its workers' compensation expenses as a result of using a captive. The only problem with Clougherty is that the insurance company is owned by the insured. As the dissent points out, this is not possible in any form under the majority's ruling. In effect, the majority has run headlong into *Moline Properties* yet achieved a different result.

*Mobil Oil* involved a large multi-national that was concerned that it was purchasing insurance inefficiently and that the purchased policies were inadequate for the risks they were covering.[558] In response to an internally generated report,[559] Mobil incorporated two captive insurance companies—

---

556    *Id.*
557    *Id.* at 951.
558    Mobil Oil Corp. v. United States, 8 Cl. Ct. 555, 557 (1985).
559    *Id.* at 557-58 (called the Adams report).

the General Overseas Insurance Company (GOIC) in the early 1960s in the Bahamas and the Bluefield Company in 1966 in Bermuda.[560] Bluefield was incorporated because of political problems in the Bahamas.[561] Both companies had their offices in their respective jurisdictions of incorporation, and both conducted their businesses in a manner consistent with insurance company practices.[562] While GOIC's initial capital was 50,000 one-pound-per-share stocks, the capital was increased to approximately $9.6 million Sterling in late 1962.[563] By 1968, Bluefield had capital of approximately $12 million.[564] Both companies were able to operate at a cheaper rate than that of comparable commercial insurance companies.[565]

> The major portions of GOIC's and Bluefield's business consisted of reinsurance of risks of Mobil Oil Corporation and its affiliates. GOIC and Bluefield normally did not write reinsurance with respect to the risks of parties other than Mobil Corporation or its affiliates, unless the risks bore some relationship to a business activity of Mobil Oil Corporation or one of its affiliates.[566]

The court did not state the exact percentage of non-Mobil business in either company's portfolio.

---

560 *Id.*
561 *Id.*
562 *Id.*
563 *Id.*
564 *Id.*
565 *Id.* at 559.
566 *Id.* at 561.

The court framed the issue as the deductibility of the premiums Mobil paid to its captives and offered an analysis of all the previous captive cases. They noted that in *Carnation*, the parent company offered to capitalize the captive with an additional $3 million if necessary.[567] This prevented the shifting of risk from the parent to the captive.[568] The court noted that the decision in *Stearns Rogers* relied on the "economic family" concept; so long as the risk of loss was contained within a corporate family, there was no risk shifting.[569] The court made the same observation regarding the parent in Beech; so long as the parent owned all the captive's stock, there could be no risk shifting.[570] In addition, the captive in Beech was undercapitalized.[571] *Crawford Fitting* was decided for the taxpayer because sufficient separation existed between the parent and the captive.[572] Finally, the court noted that the decision in *Clougherty* followed the "economic family" doctrine: no risk shifting occurred so long as the risk was transferred to a company that was a member of the same economic family.[573]

Mobil based their objection to the government's disallowance of deductions on the now familiar doctrine that this violated *Moline Properties*.[574] The court noted that the service's argument was not a violation of the separateness of corporate entities but a reclassification of the transaction, which is allowed under

---

567 *Id.* at 564.
568 *Id.*
569 *Id.* at 564-65.
570 *Id.* at 565.
571 *Id.*
572 *Id.* at 565-66.
573 *Id.* at 566.
574 *Id.* at 567.

section 482.[575] In addition, the court argued that "insurance through a wholly owned insurance affiliate is essentially the same as setting up reserve accounts."[576] The court stuck with the "balance sheet" argument and ruled for the service: "the risk of loss remains with the parent and is reflected on the balance sheet and income statements of the parent."[577]

The third situation outlined in Revenue Ruling 77-316 is the same as the first situation:

> During the taxable year domestic corporation X and its domestic subsidiaries entered into a contract for fire and other casualty insurance with S1, a newly organized wholly owned foreign "insurance" subsidiary of X. S1 was organized to insure properties and other casualty risks of X and its domestic subsidiaries. X and its domestic subsidiaries paid amounts as casualty insurance premiums directly to S1. Such amounts reflect commercial rates for the insurance involved. S1

---

[575] Id. See also 26 U.S.C. 482: "In any case of two or more organizations, trades, or businesses (whether or not incorporated, whether or not organized in the United States, and whether or not affiliated) owned or controlled directly or indirectly by the same interests, the Secretary may distribute, apportion, or allocate gross income, deductions, credits, or allowances between or among such organizations, trades, or businesses, if he determines that such distribution, apportionment, or allocation is necessary in order to prevent evasion of taxes or clearly to reflect the income of any of such organizations, trades, or businesses. In the case of any transfer (or license) of intangible property (within the meaning of section 936(h)(3)(B)), the income with respect to such transfer or license shall be commensurate with the income attributable to the intangible."

[576] *Mobil* at 567.

[577] *Id.*

has not accepted risks from parties other than X and its domestic subsidiaries.[578]

However,

> The facts are the same as set forth in Situation 1 except that domestic corporation Z and its domestic subsidiaries paid amounts as casualty insurance premiums directly to Z's wholly owned foreign "insurance" subsidiary, S3. Contemporaneous with the acceptance of this insurance risk, and pursuant to a contractual obligation to Z and its domestic subsidiaries, S3 transferred 90% of the risk through reinsurance agreements to an unrelated insurance company, W.[579]

According to the service, any amount not retained by the group is a deductible under 26 U.S.C. 162(a).[580] Therefore, under situation 3, the 90 percent transferred out of the corporate group is insurance and can therefore be deducted. The reason is this amount is not "under the control of the parent"[581] as it is under the control of a third party.

The primary case that illustrates this point is *Crawford Fitting Co. v. United States*.[582] *Crawford Fitting* involved three sets of companies. The first set was Crawford, Nupro, Whitey, and Cajon, all of which manufactured "valves and fittings ... used

---

578  Rev. Rul. 77-316.
579  *Id.*
580  *Id.*
581  *Id.*
582  *Crawford Fitting*, 606 F.Supp. 136.

in numerous applications."[583] The second set of companies was the regional warehouses that purchased the manufacturers' products. The warehouses were broken down regionally, with one warehouse each for the eastern, southern, central, and western United States.[584] Each of these warehouses sold to a group of independent and exclusive Crawford distributors.[585] Mr. Fred Lennon was the sole owner of Crawford[586] and was also a majority owner of each regional warehouse.[587] In order to obtain reasonable products and general liability insurance, the Crawford companies created Constance Insurance Company in March 1978.[588] Each regional warehouse owned 20 percent of Constance while the remaining 20 percent was owned by a Crawford executive and one attorney who did extensive work for Crawford.[589]

Constance was capitalized with $1 million and did not receive any other capital infusion.[590] Additionally, no other Crawford company or subsidiary indemnified or guaranteed Constance's payment.[591] Constance issued a general liability policy for 45 Crawford companies and 115 independent distributors.[592] Alexander wrote the policies.[593] Constance paid for Alexander's services.[594] Constance provided $1.5 million in coverage but

---

583   *Id.* at 137.
584   *Id.*
585   *Id.*
586   *Id.*
587   *Id.* at 137.
588   *Id.* at 138.
589   *Id.*
590   *Id.*
591   *Id.*
592   *Id.*
593   *Id.*
594   *Id.*

only retained $100,000 of the risk by reinsuring $1.4 million of the coverage with independent third-party insurers.[595] Crawford paid $157,028 to Constance for the year in question.[596] The service disallowed $20,485 of the deductions, arguing that this is the amount of risk that Constance retained.[597] The issue for the court was whether or not the entire payment was deductible as an insurance premium.[598]

The US argument boiled down to the now familiar "economic family" argument: any risk that remained within the same "economic family" was in fact a reserve fund and therefore not a legitimate expense for insurance.[599] The plaintiff argued that the payment was a legitimate insurance payment, because it was "an arms-length transaction, and Constance is not 'related' to Crawford."[600] However,

> [i]t is undisputed that to the extent Constance reinsured the remainder of the risk, in the amount of $1,400,000.00, with the Bermuda Fire & Marine Insurance Co., Ltd., an unrelated insurance company, plaintiff is entitled to a deduction for the insurance premium for that amount of coverage.[601]

In other words, the only point of contention was the amount of risk retained by Constance.

---

595 *Id.*
596 *Id.*
597 *Id.*
598 *Id.* at 140.
599 *Id.* at 141.
600 *Id.*
601 *Id.*

After a review of the then-decided captive cases, the court noted that Crawford was different:

> First, looking at the nature of the ownership of the plaintiff and the captive insurance company, the Court finds it is somewhat different in the case at bar than in the cases aforementioned. In this case, plaintiff Crawford Fitting Company is a separately incorporated entity from the wholly owned captive insurance company, and is not the parent company of the captive.[602]

The parent's direct ownership of the captive is the basis of the service's "economic family" argument. Under that theory, when the captive makes a payment to the parent, the captive's stock value drops. This in turn lowers the parent's assets by the amount of the captive's payment. As a result, there is in fact no risk shifting. However, in this case, the parent did not own the captive's stock. Therefore, when the captive made a payment to the parent, the parent's assets did not decrease. Hence, risk shifting did occur. The court noted,

> However, in the instant case, the Court finds that the taxpayer and the other shareholders of the captive insurance company, as well as the insureds, are not so economically related that their separate financial transactions must be aggregated and treated as the transactions of a single taxpayer, the plaintiff. The Court further finds that the economic risk of loss of the plaintiff was shifted and distributed among the

---

602  *Id.* at 145.

shareholders of the captive insurance company and its insureds.[603]

The service pointed out that the same person—Fred Lennon—owned a majority of Crawford and each warehouse.[604] However, none of the companies owned each other. While they had one common individual owner, there were non-common corporate owners. As the court explained,

> However, we note that Crawford Fitting Company, as earlier pointed out, was not the parent company of the warehouses, nor was it the parent company of the captive insurance company. The fact that Fred A. Lennon owns Crawford and a percentage of the warehouses does not mean that the warehouses' 80% ownership interest in Constance is the same as an 80% ownership by Crawford. Any gain or loss enjoyed or suffered by Constance does not affect the net worth of Crawford. The Court thus finds Fred A. Lennon's ownership interest in the different companies inconsequential where each in fact was incorporated for a valid business purpose independent from the others, and the creation of each was followed by legitimate business activity.[605]

In other words, each corporation was a unique corporation with a single individual owner. This provided all the differentiation the court needed to rule that risk shifting had occurred.

---

603  *Id.*
604  *Id.* at 146.
605  *Id.*

In addition, the large number of insureds provided risk distribution. Constance provided insurance for each Crawford company, each warehouse, 115 Crawford distributors, and several individuals associated with the Crawford companies.[606] These were each independent risks that made "the sum of the risks carried by the captive company less than the sum of the risks insured."[607] Finally, Constance was adequately capitalized, and no company provided a financial guarantee in the event Crawford was unable to meet a financial obligation.[608]

There are two structuring themes that run through the previous cases. First, a single parent cannot own a captive if the captive does not insure another company aside from the parent. This is still good law.[609] Second, spreading out ownership as done in *Crawford Fitting* is a way to mitigate the problems of direct ownership of the captive. Going forward, spreading out ownership will be important.

**Humana**

*Humana* was a groundbreaking case because it was the first major victory for a taxpayer in the captive insurance area.[610] *Humana* was (and is) a publicly traded health care company.[611] By the mid-1970s, it was incredibly difficult for the company to find adequate insurance.[612] The company considered going

---

606  *Id.* at 146-47.
607  *Id.* at 147.
608  *Id.* at 147.
609  See *Clougherty*, 84 T.C. 948.
610  *Humana*, 88 T.C. 197; and *Humana*, 881 F. 2d 247.
611  *Humana*, 88 T.C. 197, 199.
612  *Id.* at 200.

uninsured but did not have enough funds to withstand a catastrophic risk.[613] They also considered setting up a reserve, but payments to a reserve fund are not deductible, and the trust fund would not allow Humana to access the third-party insurance market.[614] A third option was combining with other hospitals in a five-year pooling arrangement, but Humana did not want to commit to a five-year program and was unsure about the financial viability of other possible participants.[615] Finally, the company could set up a captive insurance company—an option that was accepted because

> it possessed none of the perceived disadvantages associated with the other options and it would provide a regulated method of insuring risks which would both isolate funds for the settlement of claims and satisfy interested lenders, mortgagees, and securities analysts. In addition, Option (4) [establishing a captive] would provide access to world reinsurance and excess insurance markets.[616]

On August 5, 1976, Humana incorporated Health Care Indemnity under the Colorado Captive Insurance Act.[617] The Insurance Department of Colorado approved Humana's establishment of a captive under Colorado law.[618]

---

613  *Id.*
614  *Id.* 200-201.
615  *Id.* 201.
616  *Id.*
617  *Id.*
618  *Id.*

Health Care Indemnity (the captive's name) issued preferred and common shares.[619] Humana purchased all 250,000 shares of common stock by paying "$750,000 in the form of an irrevocable letter of credit issued in favor of the commissioner of insurance of the State of Colorado."[620] Each common share of stock had five votes.[621] A Humana subsidiary in the Netherlands Antilles purchased all 150,000 shares of preferred stock for $250,000.[622] There were no further agreements among Humana, its Netherlands Antilles subsidiary, and Health Care Indemnity for the injection of any additional funds into the captive insurance company.[623]

Health Care Indemnity issued three policies that covered the vast majority of Humana's hospitals.[624] All of these policies conformed with industry standard practices.[625] For years 1977 to 1979, Humana (the parent) paid total premiums of $21,055,575 to Health Care Indemnity.[626] These payments represented amounts for the parent and its subsidiaries.[627] The sole issue at trial was whether these amounts were deductible as insurance premiums.[628] However, there were two sets of premiums. The first was from the parent company to the captive. The second was from the subsidiaries to the captive. It is important to remember this distinction going forward.

---

619  *Id.* at 202.
620  *Id.*
621  *Id.*
622  *Id.*
623  *Id.*
624  *Id.* One policy covered sixty-four hospitals, a second covered fifty-nine, and a third covered ninety-seven.
625  *Id.*
626  *Id.* at 203.
627  *Id.*
628  *Id.* at 206.

Humana lost the trial case but filed a petition for reconsideration.[629] The tax court withdrew its memorandum opinion and issued a full opinion after review by the nineteen-person court.[630] The written opinion contains a twelve-member majority opinion, an eight-person concurrence, a two-member concurrence, and a seven-member dissent.[631] The sole reason for Humana's petition was to get a long opinion that the company could use for the basis of an appeal.

The court first notes the many captive cases heard before *Humana* that apply directly to the non-deductibility of premiums from a parent to a wholly owned subsidiary.[632] In this case, that would represent the payments from the Humana parent to the subsidiary. Next, the court notes "payments to a captive insurance company are equivalent to additions to a reserve for losses."[633] If these payments are not deducible as insurance payments, they are not deductible at all.[634] The court quickly dealt with this issue—the payments from the parent to the subsidiary—by citing previous cases (such as *Carnation*[635] and *Clougherty*[636]) and disallowing the deductions.[637]

The court next turns to the issue of the payments from Humana's subsidiaries to the captive, which is referred to as the brother-

---

629   *Humana,* 881 F. 2d 247, 259.
630   *Id.*
631   *Id.*
632   *Humana,* 88 T.C. 197, 206-7. See the reasoning of *Carnation* and *Clougherty* as applied to *Beech Aircraft* and *Stearns-Rogers.*
633   *Id.* at 207.
634   *Id.*
635   See *Carnation,* 71. T.C. 400.
636   *Clougherty,* 84 T.C. 948.
637   *Id.*

sister issue. In this situation, it is important to remember the logic of the non-deductibility of payments to the captive from the parent. A payment from the captive would reduce the value of the captive's stock. Because the parent owned all of the captive's stock, the captive's payment would lower the value of the parent's assets on its respective balance sheet. Therefore, there was no risk shifting according to the standard established in *Helvering v. LeGierse*. In *Humana*, the majority "extend[ed] the rationale [of *Carnation* and *Clougherty*] to the brother-sister fact pattern."[638] They did so even though none of the subsidiaries owned any of the captive's stock.

In extending the parent subsidiary rationale to the brother-sister relationship, the majority relied heavily on the expert testimony of Mr. Stewart and Dr. Plotkin—both witnesses for the government.[639] In fact, the court quoted fairly extensively from Mr. Stewart and Dr. Plotkin's joint opinion. Dr. Plotkin had testified in several other captive insurance cases. Because Dr. Plotkin's theories formed the basis of the government's argument for over twelve years, a detailed analysis is warranted. In addition, following the citation from the case, I will point out the flaws of the argument.

> Commercial insurance is a mechanism for transferring the financial uncertainty arising from pure risks faced by one firm to another in exchange for an insurance premium. Such financial uncertainty is caused by the possibility of certain types of occurrences that may have only adverse financial consequences. A

---

638   *Id.* at 208.
639   *Id.*

corporation such as Humana that places its risks in a captive insurance company that it owns, either directly or through a parent corporation, subsidiary, or a fronting company, is not relieving itself of this financial uncertainty. The reason for this is simply that such corporation, through its ownership position, still holds the benefits and burdens of retaining the financial consequences of its own risks. It has a dollar-for-dollar economic interest in the result of any "insured" peril.[640]

A firm placing its risks in a captive insurance company in which it holds a sole or predominant ownership position is not relieving itself of financial uncertainty. It is, through its ownership, retaining the burdens and benefits of assuming the financial responsibility of its own risks.[641]

This is by now a familiar argument. So long as a company owns a large enough position of the captive's stock, risk is not transferred. When the captive makes a payment, the captive's net worth drops by the value of the payment. This in turn decreases the captive's stock price, all of which is on the parent's balance sheet. This in turn lowers the parent's net worth, thereby preventing risk shifting.

However, this argument makes an important and possibly erroneous valuation assumption: that book value (assets − (liabilities + owner's equity)) is always completely reflected in

---

640   *Id.* at 209-10.
641   *Id.* at 210-11.

a stock's price. While book value can be a method of valuation, it is hardly the only one. For example, in this case, it is possible that if Humana wanted to sell the captive outright, the stock price would sell at a premium because of the captive's primary client. As a further example, consider the way publicly traded insurers trade after a natural disaster. Share prices drop, but hardly at a rate that completely reflects the expected future payout of all losses related to the catastrophe. While publicly traded insurers have far more risk distribution, the captive here insured multiple Humana subsidiaries.

The decision continues:

> A term frequently used for the act of insuring is underwriting. An essential element of the concept of underwriting is the transference of uncertainty from one firm to another, generally from the one whose activities naturally give rise to the uncertainty to one whose investors are in the business of accepting such uncertainty for the potential profit they can earn thereby.
>
> Thus, insurers, and the interests that own them, are risk takers. They assume the financial consequences of the risks for others in return for a premium payment.[642]

There is nothing in the fact pattern indicating that Humana's captive was not in the business of insuring risks. In fact, the facts state that HCI's insurance costs were developed using standard industry formula, were within standard industry

---

642   *Id.* at 209-10.

experience, and were billed using standard insurance billing methods.[643] In addition, HCI was originally capitalized with $1 million,[644] received an additional $21,055,575 in premiums over three years,[645] had payout limitations under each of the three types of policies it wrote,[646] and had reinsurance.[647] In short, the company clearly underwrote risks and was able to pay claims—thereby implying they could pay for the "financial consequences" of the policies they underwrote. This argument is based on *Moline Properties*, which requires courts to recognize a legitimately established and maintained business.[648] However, the fact that the captive was a legitimate insurance company is irrelevant under the Plotkin analysis because the parent owns a predominant share of the captive's stock.

The decision continues:

---

643 *Id.* at 203: "The foregoing charges were developed by Marsh & McLennan pursuant to standard industry practice generally by applying to the average number of occupied beds, a composite rate developed by a rating organization known as Insurance Service Offices. The resulting amounts were billed by HCI to Humana Inc. on a monthly basis and were paid by Humana Inc. in a single payment representing the total premiums for all of the hospitals. Later, by means of an allocation formula, portions of the foregoing amounts were charged to the subsidiaries."

644 *Id.* at 202.

645 *Id.* at 203.

646 *Id.* 205.

647 *Id.*

648 *Moline Properties,* 319 U.S. 436: "The doctrine of corporate entity fills a useful purpose in business life. Whether the purpose be to gain an advantage under the law of the state of incorporation or to avoid or to comply with the demands of creditors or to serve the creator's personal or undisclosed convenience, so long as that purpose is the equivalent of business activity or is followed by the carrying on of business by the corporation, the corporation remains a separate taxable entity."

A question that perplexes some when initially confronted with the captive insurance area is whether or not respondent has chosen to treat, either directly or indirectly, two separate legal entities as one single economic unit. One's first impression might be that, since a parent corporation can deal at arm's length with a subsidiary in other areas besides insurance and have such transactions respected by respondent, "insurance premiums" paid to a captive should not be treated any differently. The answer to this paradox lies in the unique nature of insurance transactions relative to other types of parent/subsidiary transactions.

True insurance relieves the firm's balance sheet of any potential impact of the financial consequences of the insured peril. For the price of the premiums, the insured rids itself of any economic stake in whether or not the loss occurs ... however as long as the firm deals with its captive, its balance sheet cannot be protected from the financial vicissitudes of the insured peril.[649]

The above paragraphs highlight the primary thrust of Plotkin's argument and the problem many companies and commentators had with the rulings in prior captive cases: they treated the captive and the parent as part of the same economic family, thereby overlooking or ignoring the captive's separate legal existence as required by the *Moline Properties* decision (and economic common sense). The court attempted to limit the *Humana* ruling to the case's facts as a way to mitigate the possible legal fallout from accepting the "economic family"

---

649  *Id.* at 211-12.

doctrine, but in the end, it did not work. The IRS's reasoning behind this theory that "the parent through its control of the corporate family members ... has control over the movement of assets within the family"[650] was legally untenable. Taken to its logical conclusion, it would allow the service to invalidate most intra-corporate transfers if desired. This is a primary reason why it was never accepted by previous courts and probably why the *Humana* court refused to adopt it as well.[651] Also, as noted above, there are plenty of ways to value a stock, indicating that the dollar-for-dollar reduction of the parent's balance sheet for a captive's payment to the parent is a questionable proposition.

At the tax court level, the *Humana* decision is best know for the partial dissent of Judge Korner, which expressly rejected the application of *Carnation* and *Clougherty* to the brother-sister relationships:

> So far as the majority opinion holds that the premiums paid to HCI by petitioner Humana, Inc. (the common

---

650 Rev. Rul. 77-316.
651 *Humana* at 213. The concurring opinion written by Judge Whitaker specifically stated the "economic family" doctrine was not needed to arrive at the case's conclusion. Instead, all the court needed to do was apply *Helvering v. LeGierse* to the current facts: "In reaching this result we have not collapsed or looked behind the separate corporate existence of any party. As the Supreme Court did LeGierse, we have merely applied to the facts before us the accepted definition of insurance and the well known 'form over substance' doctrine" (216–18). "In sum, I believe that the "economic family" theory may conflict with fundamental principles of tax law by invoking attribution among related corporations where it has not been legislated by Congress. FN3 I see no reason to give such a concept credence, as the majority is doing here. Consequently, I concur only in the result reached by the majority" (218–20).

parent corporation) for insurance ON ITSELF may not be deducted as insurance premiums, I agree that such an outcome is controlled by our holdings in *Carnation Co. v. Commissioner* and *Clougherty Packing Co. v. Commissioner*. Therefore, I concur in that portion of the opinion.

With respect to the majority's holding that the same result obtained with respect to premiums paid by the Humana subsidiaries to HCI for comparable insurance on them and their employees, I dissent.[652]

Neither *Carnation* nor *Clougherty* had a brother-sister relationship; both had a parent that wholly owned the captive. Here, Humana had many subsidiaries and a captive insurance company. But the subsidiaries had no ownership interest in the captive. As the court observed,

> Humana's insured subsidiaries owned no stock in HCI, nor vice versa. The subsidiaries' balance sheets and net worth would in no way be affected by the payment of an insured claim by HCI. It follows that when the Humana subsidiaries paid THEIR OWN premiums for THEIR OWN insurance, as the facts show, they shifted their risks to HCI. The rationale of *Carnation* and *Clougherty* thus does not apply, and such premiums should be allowable as deductions to the subsidiaries.[653]

---

652  *Id.* at 219-20.
653  *Id* at 222.

Under *Carnation* and *Clougherty*, the primary issue preventing the transferring of risk from the parent to the captive was the parent's ownership of captive stock. However, where a company does not own any stock in the insurance company, a payment from the insurance company to the insured does not impact the insured's balance sheet. Hence, there is risk shifting.

This is the key point of the *Humana* case. For the first time, part of the taxpayer's structure was accepted as valid by the court. On appeal, the court ruled thusly:

> With regard to the second issue, the brother-sister issue, we believe that the tax court incorrectly extended the rationale of Carnation and Clougherty in holding that the premiums paid by the subsidiaries of Humana Inc. to Health Care Indemnity, as charged to them by Humana Inc., did not constitute valid insurance agreements with the premiums deductible under Internal Revenue Code § 162(a) (1954). We must treat Humana Inc., its subsidiaries and Health Care Indemnity as separate corporate entities under Moline Properties. When considered as separate entities, the first prong of LeGierse is clearly met. Risk shifting exists between the subsidiaries and the insurance company. There is simply no direct connection in this case between a loss sustained by the insurance company and the affiliates of Humana Inc. as existed between the parent company and the captive insurance company in both Carnation and Clougherty.[654]

---

654  *Humana*, 881 F.2d 247, 252.

This is the logical outcome of the *Carnation* and *Clougherty* decisions. Also note the statement and acceptance of *Moline Properties*: after years of courts glossing over these decisions or attempting to limit a holding only to cases involving captive insurance, a court finally acknowledges that the captive is a separate company that must be recognized as such for tax purposes.

The court made the following salient points regarding the captive's position: the company met the minimum standard for an insurance company under Colorado law, it was adequately capitalized, it did not have an agreement with Humana for additional capital contributions, it was formed for a legitimate business purpose, and it issued insurance policies as commonly accepted in the industry.[655] In other words, there is no legal reason to rule the company is a sham or not organized for a legitimate business purpose.

In addition,

> The tax court misapplies this substance over form argument. The substance over form or economic reality argument is not a broad legal doctrine designed to distinguish between legitimate and illegitimate transactions and employed at the discretion of the tax court whenever it believes that a taxpayer is taking advantage of the tax laws to produce a favorable result for the taxpayer ... In general, absent specific congressional intent to the contrary, as is the situation in this case, a court cannot disregard a transaction in the name of economic reality and substance over form

---

655 *Id.* at 253.

absent a finding of sham or lack of business purpose under the relevant tax statute.[656]

This is another key point from the *Humana* appeal. For a majority of captive cases, the service had been dancing around the issue of sham transaction and lack of business purpose without actually making the argument. Hence, the continual use of the phrase "substance over form." Here, the appeals court takes the service and the lower courts to task for incorrectly using the substance-over-form argument.

*Humana* was a landmark decision. The company utilized a captive insurance structure[657] that is still in use today, and the appeals court finally recognized and applied *Moline Properties* appropriately.

**Gulf Oil**

*Gulf Oil* was an important decision for two reasons. First, it again highlighted that original capitalization must allow the captive to operate on its own as a separate insurance company. Second, *Gulf Oil* was one of the first cases to provide an in-depth discussion of risk distribution.[658]

The facts in *Gulf Oil* are strikingly similar to those of *Humana*.[659] Starting in the 1960s, Gulf Oil had a difficult time finding adequately priced insurance.[660] As a result, the company

---

656 *Id.* at 244-45.
657 The captive can insure the risk(s) of its brother/sister companies.
658 See *Helvering*, 312 U.S. 531, 532.
659 *Gulf Oil*, 914 F.2d 396.
660 *Id.* at 410.

decided to self-insure both through an industry consortium called Oil Insurance Ltd. and a captive insurer called Insco.[661] Although the company authorized Insco to issue 1,000 shares valued at $1,000 per share, the company sold only 12 percent of its authorized shares.[662] Insco reinsured a large number of Gulf Oil's existing insurance contracts, usually through prearranged transactions.[663] Gulf Oil would sign a contract with a primary insurance carrier, and the carrier would then cede some of the insurance risk to Insco along with some of the premium Gulf Oil paid to the insurer.[664] Additionally, Gulf Oil "executed guarantees in favor of AIG ... that obligated Gulf to indemnify [AIG] should Insco be unable to meet its obligations with regard to its reinsurance risks."[665] In 1975, Gulf Oil shifted ownership of Insco to Transocean, which contributed $880,000 in capital in addition to purchasing 9,000 shares at $1,000 per share.[666] This brought Insco's total capital to $10 million.[667] The commissioner disallowed roughly $10 million of deductions in 1974 and roughly $11 million of premiums in 1975 that were paid by Gulf Oil and its affiliates to third-party insurers and that were then ceded to Insco as reinsurance premiums.[668] Gulf Oil appealed an adverse tax court ruling.[669]

On appeal, the court upheld the lower court's decision against Gulf Oil, noting,

---

661 *Id.*
662 *Id.*
663 *Id.*
664 *Gulf Oil*, 89 T.C. 1010, 1014.
665 *Id.*
666 *Id.*
667 *Id.*
668 *Id.*
669 *Id.*

Although many of the facts in Humana are similar to those in this case, critical distinguishing facts exist. In contrast to the facts here, (1) the captive insurer in Humana was fully capitalized initially; (2) no agreement ever existed under which Humana, Inc. or any Humana subsidiary would contribute additional capital to the insurer; and (3) Humana, Inc. and the hospital subsidiaries never contributed additional amounts to the insurer nor took any steps to insure the insurer's performance.[670]

All of the above points come down to the issue of capitalization. From a structuring perspective, the lesson could not be clearer. First, initially capitalize the captive adequately. In this case, Gulf Oil initially purchased 12 percent of the authorized shares. Second—and like the plaintiff in *Carnation*—Gulf Oil indemnified the captive in the event of losses. This indicated the captive could not stand on its own and therefore may have been a sham transaction. In addition, it prevents risk shifting as required under *Helvering*. Should the parent file a claim that forces the captive to seek an additional captive from the parent, the parent would essentially pay itself. Finally, the contribution of additional capital after the forming and running of the captive indicates that the captive may have been undercapitalized at the beginning.

At the trial level, there was an extensive discussion of risk distribution[671]—an element of the *Helvering* insurance definition left out of earlier captive cases. The reason for the

---

670 *Id.* at 412.
671 *Gulf Oil*, 89 T.C. 1010.

discussion is that Insco obtained 2 percent of its premium income from non–Gulf Oil corporate family members in 1975.[672] While this amount was small, it was enough to force the court into a discussion about non-corporate family insurance business for the captive.

In the *Carnation* and *Clougherty* cases, the insurance company only insured one company—the parent. In those cases, the insurance company's risk was entirely dependent on the experiences of one company. Therefore, the courts were unwilling to rule that the captive was an insurance company, largely because "the arrangement was merely in substance the equivalent of a reserve for losses or self-insurance."[673] However, in *Gulf Oil,* there were non-parent risks present. While these represented only 2 percent of coverage provided by Insco in 1975, the amount increased to over 50 percent in 1983.[674] At some point, the court noted the law of large numbers begins to take hold. Under this theory, "the risk carried by an insurer is far less than the sum of the risks insured."[675] Put another way, "WITH AN INCREASING NUMBER OF VENTURES IN A COMBINED POOL, THE UNUSUALLY FAVORABLE AND UNUSUALLY HARMFUL EXPERIENCES TEND TO STAY MORE NEARLY IN BALANCE" (emphasis added by the court).[676]

Put another way:

---

672  *Id.* at 1025.
673  *Id.* at 1023: "The fortunes of the two entities are interlocked to the extent that the risks insured in the captive are not reinsured."
674  *Id.* at 1025.
675  *Id.* at footnote 9.
676  *Id.* at 1026.

If all of the insureds are related, the insurance is merely self-insurance, because the group's premium pool is used only to cover the group's losses. By adding unrelated insureds the pool from which losses are paid no longer is made up of only the affiliated group's premiums. When a sufficient proportion of premiums paid by unrelated parties is added, the premiums of the affiliated group will no longer cover anticipated losses of all of the insureds; the members of the affiliated group must necessarily anticipate relying on the premiums of the unrelated insureds in the event that they are "the unfortunate few" and suffer more than their proportionate share of the anticipated losses.

Thus, when the aggregate premiums paid by the captive's affiliated group is insufficient in a substantial amount to pay the aggregate anticipated losses of the entire group, the affiliates and unrelated entities, the premiums paid by the affiliated group should be deductible as insurance premiums and should no longer be characterized as payments to a reserve from which to pay losses.[677]

The above paragraph makes more sense when applied to a fact pattern. For example, company X owns a captive. Company X pays premiums to the captive. Company X files a claim with the captive. The captive pays, but the only money the captive has was provided by the parent—the company receiving payments. Hence, there is no risk distribution, because the parent's risks are not spread over the risks of other companies. Hence there is no insurance.

---

677  *Id.* at 1026.

Let us add ten different companies to the pool of risk, all of which pay the same premium to the insurance company. Now, when company X files a claim with the captive, the captive probably pays some of company X's claim with non–company X money—that is, money provided to the captive by another company. The court is noting that at some point, enough companies contribute to the pool used to pay claims that the pool no longer provides self-insurance (paying claims only with money contributed by the parent) but instead provides real insurance (because the money used to pay the claims comes from other participants in the insurance pool).

The court continued:

> With these principles in mind we turn to the facts of the present case. For the year 1974, the facts of this case are in all material respects the same as those in our prior decisions, and therefore those decisions control. The amounts paid to Insco by Gulf and its affiliates are not deductible as insurance premiums. With respect to the year 1975, we reach the same result for the same reasons, with one noted difference. We have considered Insco's unrelated business in order to determine whether it is sufficient to affect the premium pool such that risk transfer has occurred, and have concluded that we do not have enough facts to determine the same. However, even without additional evidence we have concluded that the addition of 2% of unrelated premiums is de minimis and would not satisfy us that risk transfer has occurred. We reserve

judgment however on years other than those before the Court.[678]

This paragraph provided an important point. First, for the court to accept the captive as a legitimate insurance company under the law, it had to have more than 2 percent of its business come from a non-parent. This provided a starting point from a planning perspective. While 2 percent is obviously far too small, it does indicate that at some percentage, the court would recognize the captive as an insurance company. Conversely, at the upper end of the spectrum, the court stated in footnote 14, "However, if at least 50% [of the captive's insurance premiums] are unrelated [to the parent], we cannot believe that sufficient risk transfer would not be present."[679]

Now planners only had to find that percentage between those two numbers.

At the appellate level, the court also raised the possibility of the captive insuring a certain amount of non-parent risk:

> We need not reach the issue which divided the judges of the Tax Court – whether the addition of unrelated insurance premiums into the insurance pool for tax year 1975 establishes risk transfer and justifies the deduction of insurance premiums paid by the unrelated party to the insurance pool.[680]

---

678  *Id.* at 1027-28.
679  *Id.* at footnote 14.
680  *Gulf Oil*, 914 F.2d 396, 412.

More specifically, the court sidestepped the issue, which opened the door for further appeals.

**Harper**

*Harper* is an important case because the court applied a new and more comprehensive three-prong test to analyze the fact pattern. This test would become the standard benchmark of analysis in all future captive insurance cases. From a structuring perspective, it stands for the proposition that the captive must be a stand-alone and legitimately organized insurance company.

The Harper Company was a California holding company whose subsidiaries primarily engaged in international shipping.[681] Harper had a captive insurance company named Rampart.[682] Two Harper subsidiaries owned Rampart: CAC owned 40 percent, while Harper Robinson owned 60 percent.[683] Harper formed Rampart in 1974 as a Hong Kong company.[684] Rampart was subject to Hong Kong corporate law and the Hong Kong Insurance Registry.[685] Rampart "conducted its business in a manner consistent with its status as a separate corporation"[686]—it "maintained its own books of account, business records, bank accounts, and investments. Rampart shared facilities and employees with WFNE, and reimbursed WFNE therefore."[687] Rampart was solely liable for its insurance liabilities; Harper provided no "guaranty, security, reinsurance,

---

681 *Harper*, 96 T.C. 45, 47.
682 *Id.*
683 *Id.*
684 *Id.* at 49.
685 *Id.*
686 *Id.*
687 *Id.* at 50.

bond or other financial arrangement with respect to Rampart's obligations."[688] To that end, the company maintained reserves and reinsurance.[689] From the years 1974 to 1983, Rampart received premiums from non-Harper companies. The lowest percentage of premiums from non-Harper companies occurred in 1982 when 32 percent of Rampart's income came from unrelated parties.[690]

At trial, Harper presented two experts. Dr. DeVito testified that Rampart's insurance rates were "reasonable and competitive."[691] Dr. Doherty testified

> that risk transfer and risk distribution are two sides of the same coin.[692]
>
> Under his view, through the premium pooling process, related and unrelated insureds transfer their risk into a common pool securing the benefit of risk reduction. Dr. Doherty opined that in the instant case both the unrelated and related parties acquired insurance from Rampart since risk transfer and distribution occurred.[693]

The service again relied on the opinion of Dr. Plotkin, who advanced the now familiar argument that risk shifting does not occur between a parent and wholly owned captive insurance

---

688  *Id.*
689  *Id.* at 53.
690  *Id.* at 52.
691  *Id.* at 54.
692  *Id.* at 59.
693  *Id.* at 55.

company.[694] In addition, he testified that the addition of non-parent risks actually increases "the risk of ruin or insolvency" for the captive.[695]

The court introduced a new three-prong test to determine "the propriety of claimed insurance deductions by a parent or affiliated company to a captive insurance company."[696] The three prongs are the following:

(1) whether the arrangement involves the existence of an "insurance risk";
(2) whether there was both risk shifting and risk distribution; and
(3) whether the arrangement was for "insurance" in its commonly accepted sense.[697]

In addition,

> the tax treatment of an alleged insurance payment by a parent or affiliated company to a captive insurance company is to be governed by (1) the facts and circumstances of the particular case, and (2) principles of Federal taxation, rather than economic and risk management theories.[698]

Regarding the first point, the court noted, "Basic to any insurance transaction must be risk. An insured faces some hazard; an

---

694  *Id.*
695  *Id.* at 56.
696  *Id.* at 58.
697  *Id.*
698  *Id.* at 57.

insurer accepts a premium and agrees to perform some act if or when the loss event occurs."[699] This is a fairly easy point to prove, as all companies face at least general liability. The second point is further codification of *Helvering*, which was explained earlier. Regarding the third point, the court will look at the facts to determine if the company was in fact a legitimate insurance company. In this case, the court analyzed the facts thusly:

> Rampart was organized and operated as an insurance company. It was regulated by the Insurance Registry of Hong Kong. The adequacy of Rampart's capitalization is not in dispute. The premiums charged by Rampart to its affiliates, as well as to its shippers, were the result of arm's-length transactions. The policies issued by Rampart were valid and binding. In sum, such polices were insurance policies and the arrangements between the Harper domestic subsidiaries and Rampart constituted insurance, in the commonly accepted sense.[700]

In other words, courts will now look at the entire insurance structure to determine if the company is a legitimate, stand-alone insurer. If so, it will pass the *Harper* test.

The court's ruling is clear and succinct. First, risk shifting occurred because insurance contracts were written which were sold at arm's-length prices, and the corporation that sold them (Rampart) was separate from Harper affiliates and not a sham.[701] Rampart was regulated as an insurance company

---

699   *Id.* at 58.
700   *Id.* at 60.
701   *Id.* at 59.

under the Hong Kong authority.[702] Second, risk distribution occurred: "Here, [a] relatively large number of unrelated insureds comprise approximately 30% of Rampart's business; such a level of unrelated insureds, in our opinion, constitutes a sufficient pool of insureds to provide risk distribution."[703]

This case provides several important rules. The first is the three-prong test mentioned above, which would become the bedrock of future captive analysis. In addition, the test would shift the focus to the actual workings of the captive; that is, did the captive actually operate like a bona fide insurance company? This is a more business-friendly analysis. Not one of the most famous captive cases involved anything close to tax evasion. Instead, all the businesses were looking to lower their business expenses in a legitimate way. Therefore, analyzing the transaction as a business transaction makes far more sense. Second, the inclusion of at least 30 percent of non-parent insurance business will lead to risk distribution. Going forward to the cases that follow, this will be a key point. Businesses that established captives were starting to include non-parents in the captive's risk portfolio, most likely as a way to insure that premiums were deductible. Also of importance is the collapsing of the risk shifting and risk distribution analysis as mentioned in Dr. Doherty's testimony. This allowed the court to expedite its analysis by focusing on the company's legal status, whether it was a legitimate company and whether the company was subjected to an insurance regulator. Later courts would use the same methodology to establish the existence of risk shifting and risk distribution.

---

702 *Id.*
703 *Id.* at 59-60.

On appeal, the court separated the then existing captive cases thusly:

> Prior cases which have found true insurance have also included higher percentages of unrelated business than those found here. See *Sears Roebuck & Co. v. Commissioner*, 972 F.2d 858, 860 (7th Cir.1992) (99.75% from others) and *Ocean Drilling & Exploration Co. v. United States*, 24 Cl.Ct. 714, 730 (1991) (44% to 66% from others).
>
> Cases which have found no true insurance have found much lower percentages of unrelated business. See, e.g. *Beech Aircraft Corp. v. United States*, 797 F.2d 920, 921-22 (10th Cir.1986) (0.5% from others); *Gulf Oil Corp. v. Commissioner*, 89 T.C. 1010, 1028 (1987) (2% from others), rev'd in part on other grounds, 914 F.2d 396 (3d Cir.1990); *Clougherty Packing Co. v. Commissioner*, 811 F.2d 1297, 1299 (9th Cir.1987) (none from others).
>
> Thus, it is undoubtedly true that the existence of insurance is obvious in some cases. Moreover, there is a point at which the amount of outside business is insubstantial, so true insurance does not exist.
>
> The Tax Court found that the point of insubstantiality had not been reached in this case. We cannot say that it committed clear error in so deciding.[704]

---

704  *Harper*, 979 F.2d 1341, 1342.

From the appellate court's perspective, there is clearly a point at which there is not enough outside insurance, thereby preventing risk distribution. However, 30 percent is clearly not that level.

The next four cases—*Sears, Ocean Drilling, Amerco,* and *Malone and Hyde*—are important for several reasons. First, companies now presented far more sophisticated cases at trial. Previously, they attempted to rely almost solely on *Moline Properties*. Now—thanks to the three-prong *Harper* test—companies were able to present a far more comprehensive case at trial. Second, in two cases (*Sears* and *Amerco*), the service was clearly overreaching in its attempted application of the "economic family" doctrine. Third, courts are now far more sophisticated and even handed in their analysis. In the initial cases such as *Carnation*, *Beech Aircraft*, and *Clougherty*, the courts relied almost exclusively on the IRS's case to make their decisions. Now, the courts were looking at the totality of the situation to determine if a captive was a legitimate company. In short, these cases represent a fundamental shift in the balance of power between taxpayers and the service in the realm of captive insurance litigation.

### Sears

At the time of the case, Sears was the world's largest retailer.[705] Allstate was a wholly owned Sears subsidiary and was the second largest property and liability insurer in the United States.[706] Sears purchased a variety of insurance products from Allstate.[707]

---

705   *Sears Roebuck*, 96 T.C. 61, 63.
706   *Id.* at 64.
707   These included casualty/liability, automobile/garage liability, workers' compensation, and enterprise automobile policy.

Sears's policies with Allstate comprised approximately 0.25 percent to 1 percent of Allstate's total premiums for the years in issue (1980–1982). Allstate insured between 10 percent and 15 percent of Sears's insurance risks for the years in question.[708] For the fiscal years 1980–1982, the IRS determined deficiencies related to Sears's payment of insurance premiums to Allstate. Sears contested the deficiency judgments.

At trial, the service presented a now familiar argument:

> A parent corporation can never shift risk to an insurance company which it wholly owns, regardless of the fact that a substantial part of the subsidiary's business consists of the insurance of unrelated third-party risks. All other facts are irrelevant.[709]

The service outlined its argument to Sears in Revenue Ruling 88-72.[710] In that ruling, the captive insurer was "engaged in the trade or business of issuing insurance contracts to the general public."[711] The contracts issued to the parent and its subsidiaries were a "small fraction of the captive's total business."[712] Yet in that revenue ruling, facts did not alter the basic problem of captive insurance from the service's perspective:

> For these reasons, risk shifting between X (or its subsidiaries) and S1 is not created by the existence of what is called "risk distribution." Even though

---

708 *Sears Roebuck*, 96 T.C. at 63.
709 *Id.* at 91.
710 Rev. Rul. 88-72.
711 *Id.*
712 *Id.*

unrelated third parties have successfully shifted their risks to S1 and thus disposed of their economic stakes in whether their losses occur, X continues to have an economic stake in whether its own loss or its subsidiaries' losses occur. By operating an insurance business in which it insures unrelated parties, S1 may increase the predictability of the average loss incurred on each risk and may attract additional resources that can be used to pay the loss claims of X or its subsidiaries. The increased predictability of average loss incurred and the availability of these extra resources, however, does not alter the fact that, unlike the case where there is true insurance, X is made poorer if either X or its subsidiaries experience losses. This is because the loss reduces the net worth of S1, and the net worth of X reflects the reduction in the value of S1. Thus, the risk of those losses has not been shifted to S1.[713]

The service still argued that a payment from the captive to the parent would lower the captive's stock price, leading to a decrease in value of the parent's balance sheet, thereby preventing risk shifting from occurring. Under the service's argument, no amount of non-parent business would alter this outcome.

The service again based its overall position on the "economic family" theory advanced in Revenue Ruling 77-316.[714] At trial, Dr. Plotkin again testified for the service.[715] The court provided the following synopsis of his testimony:

---

713  *Id.*
714  *Id.*
715  *Id.* at 93.

> So long as the firm does not transfer to an unrelated entity the ultimate responsibility for the financial consequences of its pure risk, it remains the risk bearer and faces the uncertainty of each year's actual financial losses. The attempted placing of a firm's pure risk, directly or indirectly, in its insurance affiliate does not accomplish a transfer of risk, nor does it constitute an insurance transaction as a matter of insurance theory or practice or as a matter of economic reality. Such arrangements should not be characterized as insurance transactions. When a firm's captive insures unrelated business, the firm has not transferred away its own pure or business risk, it has not reduced its total financial risk; rather, the firm has increased its business and total risk.[716]

No amount of non-company business will shift the risk.[717] Therefore, there could never be insurance between a parent and a captive as defined in the case law.

Sears makes one argument that is now familiar: the service's position directly contradicts the holding in *Moline Properties*—that the courts must recognize separate corporate entities so long as the companies are not shams.[718]

In addition, Sears noted,

---

716  *Id.*
717  *Sears Roebuck*, 96 T.C. at 92: "Respondent labels as 'irrelevant' all facts and circumstances other than the parent's ownership of the subsidiary."
718  *Id.* at 94.

> Allstate is a recognized insurance company, not a "captive insurer." Allstate was created to produce insurance products for the public, not to serve the risk management needs of Sears. Allstate has thousands of employees who provide insurance services for millions of policyholders. Allstate is subject to the stringent government regulations of a fully licensed insurance company. It is a financial intermediary, pooling the risk exposures and premiums of Sears together with millions of other insureds.[719]

Sears accounted for a negligible amount of Allstate's total coverage for the years in question—between 0.25 percent and 1 percent.[720] This is by far the least amount of exposure to a parent of any captive case to date. In addition, the sheer size of Allstate—"thousands of employees" and "millions of policyholders"—places this case out of the realm of previous captive cases. Also note that the petitioner is using Allstate's regulation by "stringent government regulations" as a way to imply the existence of a separate corporate entity under *Moline Properties*.

Sears continued by listing five requirements that an insurance policy from a valid insurance company must have to distinguish the company from a captive insurance company. The point of these factors was to outline a specific set of tests for the court to use in determining whether or not a captive was in fact a bona fide insurance company that must be recognized at law:

---

719  *Id.* at 95.
720  *Id.* at 61.

(1) There is a transfer of pure risk in form. In other words, legal liability with respect to specific exposures of the parent is transferred to the insurance subsidiary under an insurance policy whose form is in accord with the customs and practices in the insurance industry for the relevant line of insurance.

(2) The transfer has a substantive effect different from self-insurance,
   (a) The insuring subsidiary is subject to the network of rules regulating insurance companies.
   (b) The exposures and premiums of multiple insureds are pooled within the insuring subsidiary.
   (c) The insuring subsidiary is engaged in the business of insurance and performs an operating function normally performed by insurance companies, including the provision of such services as risk assessment and claims management.[721]

Point number one is simply another definition of risk transfer as outlined in *Helvering*: another entity aside from the parent is now legally liable when the insured event occurs. Also notice that the policy must conform to the "customs and practices [of] the insurance industry for the relevant line of insurance."[722] The existence of this factor simply bolsters the petitioner's claim of the existence of risk transfer—if the policy conforms to industry standards, then it stands a higher probability of being insurance.

Factors (2)(a) and (2)(c) are structural factors of the captive which must be present. Under condition (a), the captive must

---

721   *Id.* at 95.
722   *Id.*

be subjected to some type of regulation. This is not difficult to achieve as most jurisdictions have some type of insurance commissioner. Condition (c) simply requires the company to act as a traditionally understood insurance company. Finally, condition (b) requires the company to have risk distribution as required under *Helvering*. Finally, condition (2) simply states that the reasoning from the reserve cases does not apply to the facts.

These factors are a more detailed list than the three points listed in *Harper*,[723] which contained the following three-prong test (along with the more stringent test stated in *Sears*):

1.) Whether the arrangement involves the existence of insurance risk. This corresponds to point number 1 of the Sears court.
2.) Whether there was risk shifting and risk distribution. This corresponds to points (1) and 2(b) of the Sears court.
3.) Whether the arrangement was "insurance" in its commonly accepted sense.[724] This corresponds to points 2(a) and 2(c) of the Sears court.

Once the court explained the petitioner's and respondent's positions, it launched into a quick analysis, which corresponded to the factors of the *Harper* case.

From the outset, the court clearly stated it would take a different tact in its analysis:

---

723 *Harper*, 96 T.C. 45, 58.
724 *Harper*, 96 T.C. at 58.

the Tax Court's position has been to consider all of the facts and circumstances to determine whether a transaction nominally labeled "insurance" should be recharacterized as "self-insurance" or as some other arrangement negating the transfer of risk.[725]

As such, the court took a more holistic view of the situation, adopting the *Harper* court's three-prong test, in addition to the further clarification of the *Harper* test submitted by the petitioner. First, there clearly was insurance risk.[726] Allstate agreed to pay claims in the event of an insurable incident.[727] The terms and conditions corresponded to generally accepted concepts of insurance as understood in the insurance industry.[728] Second, the policies between Sears and Allstate shifted the risk from Sears to Allstate.[729] "Insurance contracts were written, premiums transferred, and losses paid."[730] Allstate was a separate entity not formed for the intention of insuring only Sears:[731] "Allstate was formed for a business purpose and functioned as a business apart from its parent's business."[732] Third, there was clearly risk distribution because of the breadth and scope of Allstate's insurance business."[733] Finally,

---

725 *Sears Roebuck*, 96 T.C. at 96.
726 *Sears Roebuck*, 96 T.C. at 100.
727 *Id.*
728 *Id.*
729 *Id.*
730 *Id.*
731 *Id.*
732 *Id.* at 101. The court expressly cited *Moline Properties* as the reason for this part of the ruling.
733 *Id.*

petitioner ... established through its expert testimony, and respondent does not seriously dispute, that the arrangements between Sears and Allstate are characterized as insurance for essentially all nontax purposes. A special rule for tax purposes is not justified by either statute or case law.[734]

Notice the court's reliance on Sears clearly establishing that the relationship between the two companies was insurance according to industry standards and commonly accepted notions. It is possible that given the size of Allstate, simply establishing this fact was all the court was looking for. However, unlike the earlier cases, the court was clearly looking at the overall arrangement to determine whether or not insurance existed. This is in line with the change of analytical tact since the *Humana* case, where the court started to analyze the overall situation as opposed to just whether or not the parent owned the captive's stock.

The service stood no chance on appeal. First, the appellate court did not side with the interpretation of *Helvering v. LeGierse* as offering a firm definition of insurance, instead noting, "[T]he holding of LeGierse is only that paying the 'underwriter' more than it promises to return in the event of a casualty is not insurance by any standard."[735] In other words, the court would look at the overall facts and circumstances to determine whether or not insurance existed.

---

734 *Id.*
735 *Sears Roebuck*, 972 F.2df 858, 861.

Regarding the existence of risk shifting, the court offered the following point:

> Joseph E. Stiglitz, professor of economics at Stanford, one of the leading students of risk and insurance, and an expert witness for Sears, put things nicely in saying that insurance does not shift risk so much as the pooling transforms and diminishes risk.[736]

First, note the court is favorably citing the petitioner's expert. More importantly, the court is looking less at the element of risk shifting and more at the element of risk distribution—that is, analyzing the case from the insurance company's perspective. This is in direct contradiction to the earlier captive cases where the courts were intently focused on risk transfer. The court continued:

> Allstate furnishes Sears with the same hedging and administration services it furnishes to all other customers. It establishes reserves, pays state taxes, participates in state risk sharing pools (for insolvent insurers), and so on, just as it would if Sears were an unrelated company. States recognize the transaction as "real" insurance for purposes of mandatory-insurance laws (several of the policies were purchased to comply with such laws for Sears' auto fleet and for workers' compensation in Texas). From Allstate's perspective this is real insurance in every way. It must maintain the reserves required by state law (not to mention prudent management). Sears cannot withdraw these

---

736   *Id.* at 862.

reserves on whim, and events that affect their size for good or ill therefore do not translate directly to Sears' balance sheet.[737]

In effect, Allstate was providing standard insurance services to Sears. Allstate had a claims department, it paid taxes, and it placed Sears's risk into a pool with other companies' risks. Also note the court's reliance on state's insurance regulators and regulations as a reason to approve the transaction. Harkening back to the appellate court's analysis of *Helvering*, the court was looking at the overall facts and circumstances of the overall situation to determine whether or not to approve or reclassify the transaction. To that end:

> Suppose we ask not "What is insurance?" but "Is there adequate reason to recharacterize this transaction?," given the norm that tax law respects both the form of the transaction and the form of the corporate structure. It follows from putting the matter this way that the decision of the Tax Court must be affirmed. For whether a transaction possesses substance independent of tax consequences is an issue of fact – something the Commissioner harps on when she prevails in the Tax Court. E.g. Yosha, 861 F.2d at 499 (citing cases). The transaction between Sears and Allstate has some substance independent of tax effects. It increases the size of Allstate's pool and so reduces the ratio between expected and actual losses; it puts Allstate's reserves at risk; it assigns claims administration to persons with a comparative advantage at that task. These effects are

---

737  *Id.*

> no less real than those of loans and interest payments within corporate groups – which the Commissioner usually respects even though they are occasionally recharacterized as contributions to capital.[738]

Essentially, there is no good reason for the appellate to overturn the trial court. The transaction has all of the hallmarks of an insurance situation. Sears paid premiums. When they filed a claim with Allstate, Allstate investigated the claim. By accepting a premium payment from Sears, Allstate was placing its overall capital position at risk. In short, this walks and talks like an insurance transaction, and there is no reason not to treat the transaction in a similar manner.

**Ocean Drilling**

Ocean Drilling was originally formed to take advantage of the opening of the Gulf of Mexico to oil and gas exploration.[739] "During the 1960s, plaintiff [Ocean] faced difficulties insuring its drilling rigs."[740] To deal with this issue, Ocean formed a captive insurance company in Bermuda named Mentor in 1968.[741] Ocean originally capitalized Mentor with $200,000—the minimum allowed under Bermudan law.[742] Ocean increased this amount to $950,000 in 1969 in order to attract non-Ocean business.[743] By 1974 and 1975 (the eventual years in question), Mentor had a capital surplus

---

738  *Id.* at 864.
739  *Ocean*, 988 F.2d 1135, 1138.
740  *Id.*
741  *Id.*
742  *Id.* at 1139.
743  *Id.*

of $12,508,417 and $415,943,790, respectively.[744] Mentor's office had been located in Bermuda since 1968.[745] Mentor retained accounting and legal services from Bermudan firms.[746] Mentor's books were transferred to Bermuda in 1968 and were maintained by a chartered accountant.[747] Mentor started to write non-Ocean policies in 1970.[748] Mentor's Bermudan office performed "hiring, firing, budgeting, underwriting and expanding business."[749] Mentor had five to six employees in Bermuda to perform these functions for the years 1975 and 1976.[750] Mentor charged Ocean based on commercial rates in London.[751] Mentor could refuse to insure Ocean's claims.[752] In addition, Mentor had an experienced claims adjustor who processed Ocean and non-Ocean claims.[753]

Regarding Mentor's financial accounts,

> Mentor's funds were separate from plaintiff's funds through 1975; Mentor never loaned money to plaintiff or its subsidiaries; Mentor's funds were never used as collateral for plaintiff's loans; Mentor never invested in any of plaintiff's non-insurance subsidiaries; and Mentor's investment funds were not commingled with plaintiff's investment funds. The only guarantee by

---

744 *Id.*
745 *Id.*
746 *Id.* at 1140.
747 *Id.* at 1139.
748 *Id.*
749 *Id.* at 1140.
750 *Id.*
751 *Id.* at 1142.
752 *Id.*
753 *Id.*

plaintiff of amounts payable under a Mentor policy of insurance was for a policy issued to Ben ODECO Limited ("Ben ODECO") in 1977. However, for both tax years 1974 and 1975, plaintiff included the revenue and income of Mentor on its Consolidated Statements of Income and included Mentor as an asset on its Consolidated Balance Sheets.[754]

Mentor was not completely separate from Ocean:

> Mentor was required to obtain approval from plaintiff's board of directors for certain facets of its business, including approval of its operating budget, approval of letters of credit over a certain amount, approval of large claims, and approval of capital expenditures. Furthermore, Mentor had directors and officers who were employees of plaintiff and its affiliates. In 1974 four of Mentor's seven officers were employees of plaintiff or its affiliates, and in 1975 four of Mentor's eight officers were employees of plaintiff. The treasurer for both plaintiff and Mentor, Mr. Vaughan, is an example of an individual with loyalties to both plaintiff and Mentor.[755]

However, Mentor had great latitude for its day-to-day operations. Finally, for the years in question (1974–1975), Mentor obtained 57 percent and 56 percent of its premiums from non-Ocean business.

---

754  *Id.* at 1141.
755  *Id.*

After analyzing previous captive cases, the court began its opinion:

> This court must adhere to the principles of *LeGierse* and *Moline Properties* in reaching a decision. Plaintiff and Mentor must be considered as separate entities in evaluating whether the transactions between the two companies resulted in risk shifting and risk distributing. However, if the business operations of Mentor are a sham, Mentor's "corporate form may be disregarded." *Moline Properties,* 319 U.S. at 439, 63 S.Ct. at 1134. Furthermore, even if plaintiff and Mentor are separate entities, if plaintiff retained the risk of the losses against which it insured, plaintiff's premiums amounted to a reserve for losses, and plaintiff would not be entitled to deduct such premiums from taxable income.[756]

With the previous statement in mind, consider the steps outlined in *Harper*:

1.) Whether the arrangement involves the existence of "insurance risk";
2.) Whether there was both risk shifting and risk distribution; and
3.) Whether the arrangement was for "insurance" in its commonly accepted sense.[757]

The court's determination of whether the captive is a sham satisfies two prongs of the *Harper* test—whether there was

---

756   *Id.* at 1150-51.
757   *Harper,* 96 T.C. 45, 58.

"insurance risk" and whether the transaction conformed to "commonly accepted notions of insurance."[758]

First, the court noted that the insured faced real hazards such as hurricanes and accidents.[759] The parties understood that they were purchasing insurance.[760] The parties signed contracts and paid premiums based on existing commercial rates.[761] The captive paid claims from separate accounts and was adequately capitalized.[762] The captive investigated claims before paying them.[763] In short, Mentor was a valid insurance company.

Regarding whether there was risk shifting and risk distribution, the court offered the following analysis. First, the court noted that previous courts had not defined "insurance risk."[764] To define this term, the court relied on Ocean's expert, who testified,

> An insured party pays a premium that is expected to cover the average loss. Therefore, the insured party does not transfer the cost of the average loss, since the insured party pays that amount to the insurer. What the insured party transfers to the insurer when it pays premiums is the cost of variability in losses. The risk that the insured transfers to the insurer is the variability of loss, not the complete loss from an event, such as a hurricane or an accident, since the

---

758   *Ocean,* at 1151.
759   *Id.*
760   *Id.*
761   *Id.*
762   *Id.*
763   *Id.*
764   *Id.*

insured pays a premium that covers the average cost of the complete loss.[765]

In short, the insured is preventing variability in its revenue stream from unforeseen events. For example, here Ocean is insuring against hurricane damages to its offshore gulf platforms. In the event of a hurricane, Ocean would file a claim with Mentor, which Mentor would pay. Without this payment, Ocean's earnings would suffer an extraordinary hit in the year of the hurricane's occurrence. However, with insurance, Ocean is able to mitigate the effects of a random event on the company's bottom line. In effect, Ocean has transferred the "variability of its losses" to the insurance company.

If the captive insured only the parent, then the risk the parent transferred would equal the risk the parent retained, and there would be no transfer of risk and therefore no insurance.[766] This is because the captive's stock price would drop by an amount equal to the captive's payment to the parent. This would in turn lower the parent's total assets on its balance sheet, thereby making the payment self-insurance. However, the presence of non-company insureds in the captive's risk pool furthers the insured's aim of lowering its exposure to risk by diversifying the parent's risk with a pool of non-company risk.[767] This allows the parent to transfer more risk than it retains, and therefore gives the parent a legitimate deduction for insurance under section 162. To continue the previous example, previous captive cases found risk distribution when

---

765  *Id.* at 1151–52.
766  *Id.*
767  *Id.* at 1152.

the captive received premiums from 30 percent to 99 percent of non-parent companies.[768] In all of these cases, the pool of risk the captive insured was large and diverse enough so that a payment to the parent would not cause a dollar-for-dollar reduction in the captive's stock price—and hence a dollar-for-dollar reduction on the parent's balance sheet.

The court in *Ocean* took a workman-like approach to the issue of captive insurance. First, it noted the company was a real insurance company—it performed all the requisite functions of an insurance company and did so for the parent and non-parent insureds alike. Next, the captive adequately diversified its pool of risk so that a payment from the captive to the parent could not be classified as self-insurance. The court noted that so long as the captive obtained at least 30 percent of its premiums from a non-parent/corporate family, there was sufficient risk distribution for the insurance to exist.

At this stage of the captive insurance game, the business community had effectively and completely changed the court's method of analyzing these cases. Courts now routinely looked at the insurance company's operations to determine if the company was in fact a legitimate insurance company. In addition, parent companies were far savvier regarding setting up a captive. Notice that captives now operate as legitimate insurance companies with fairly significant non-parent risks. This is one of the key developing points.

---

768  *Id.* at 1152.

**Amerco**

Amerco was a holding company for the U-Haul system.[769] It held the stock for approximately 25,000 separate U-Haul subsidiaries in the years in question.[770] Republic was a "third tier" insurance company of the Amerco system[771] and was a fully licensed property and casualty insurance company.[772] It issued a variety of policies to Amerco, including workers' compensation, general corporate insurance, U-Haul rental system policies, and "Safe Store" policies.[773] Republic had an increasing number of employees in both its insurance division and claims division.[774] For the years in question (1979–1985), non–U-Haul insurance accounted for between 54 percent and 73 percent of Republic's total business.[775]

At trial, the petitioners presented the testimony of Bruce Foudree, whom the court admitted as an expert in state insurance regulation largely because he was a former regulator.[776] His purpose was to demonstrate that Republic's insurance contracts were valid, recognized insurance contracts within the meaning of insurance as understood by state regulators.[777] The court agreed with this assessment.[778] The purpose of this testimony was to establish clearly that Republic issued industry

---

769 Amerco and Subsidiaries and Republic Western Insurance Company v. C.I.R., 96 T.C. 18, 20 (1991).
770 *Amerco*, 979 F.2d 162, 163.
771 *Id.*
772 *Amerco*, 979 F.2d at 18.
773 *Id.*
774 *Id.* at 22.
775 *Amerco*, 96 T.C. at 29.
776 *Id.* at 32.
777 *Id.*
778 *Id.*

standard insurance contracts—in other words, that Republic was a legitimate insurance company. This corresponded to the analysis outlined in the *Harper* case.[779] Amerco presented two other experts (Dr. Cummins and Neil Doherty) who testified regarding the "pooling aspect of insurance."[780] In other words, the captive's parent must place its risk with other non-parent companies' risks in order for insurance to exist. This also corresponded to another aspect of the three-prong test outlined in *Harper*.[781]

The service again used Dr. Plotkin, who advanced the "economic family" theory.[782]

After an analysis of the case law (especially *Helvering v. LeGierse*[783]), the court analyzed the facts using the three-prong test outlined in *Harper*. First, the petitioner clearly faced insurance risk.[784] As a large company with over 250 subsidiaries and a primary business of renting moving vehicles, it is clear insurance risk was present.

The court ruled that risk shifting occurred in both form and substance. That conclusion came from the fact of the transactions: "Insurance contracts were written, premiums

---

779 *Harper*, 96 T.C. 45, 58: "The following three-prong test must be applied ... whether the arrangement was for 'insurance' in its commonly accepted sense."
780 *Id.* at 33.
781 *Harper*, 96 T.C. at 58: "whether these were risk shifting and risk distribution."
782 *Amerco*, 96 T.C. at 34.
783 *Id.* at 39.
784 *Id.* at 39.

transferred and losses paid."[785] This is one of the reasons why Amerco submitted the testimony of the former state insurance regulator, Bruce Foudree. In addition, Republic was a separate entity entirely able to pay its claims.[786] In fact, Republic was rated by A.M. Best, a testament to its financial health.[787] Risk distribution was present, as Republic's insurance business was "diverse, multi-faceted and, as stated, involved a substantial amount of outside risk."[788]

Finally, the insurance contracts were clearly insurance as commonly understood. The fact that Republic was regulated by a state regulator was a key issue here, as was the sum total of the preceding analysis. Simply put, Republic was a bona fide insurance company that issued insurance policies, paid on those policies when a claim was filed, and was subjected to state regulation. The company wrote non-parent business in a large enough percentage (54 percent and 73 percent during the years in question) that risk distribution and risk shifting occurred.

On appeal, the court quickly dealt with two points—whether insurance risk existed and whether Republic was a legitimate insurance company:

> Here, as the Tax Court determined, there was an insurance risk involved the AMERCO Group undoubtedly faced potential hazards from its operations which constituted insurable risks. By

---

785  *Id.* at 40.
786  *Id.*
787  *Id.*
788  *Id.*

the same token, there could be no real doubt that Republic was engaged in the insurance business in the commonly accepted sense. The Commissioner does not contest those determinations. Thus, we must turn to an analysis of risk shifting and risk distributing.[789]

After noting that early captive cases involved captives who only insured their parents' risks,[790] the court notes this case involved a captive that wrote a substantial amount of non-parent business.[791] While the IRS did not think this an important fact,[792] the court noted the tax court did not agree with the service's analysis when non-parent risks are insured by the captive.[793] In other words, the presence of non-parent risks was exceedingly important in this case's analysis. As this court noted,

> [A]s the Tax Court noted in a related case, "risk transfer and risk distribution are two sides of the same coin which as an integrated whole constitute 'insurance.'" That is to say, when the pool consists of a substantial amount of dollars, and risk, from those outside the parent and its affiliates, there is a true shift of the risk, even though the parent could suffer somewhat if the captive made a payment on account of an insured's loss. In a real sense, the parent's risk has been placed with the captive and thence spread among all of those in the pool.

---

789 *Amerco,* 979 f.2d at 165.
790 *Id.* at 166.
791 *Id.*
792 See Rev. Rul 88-72.
793 *Amerco,* 96 T.C. at 166.

The Commissioner claims that this improperly collapses the ideas of risk shifting and risk distributing. What the Commissioner does not recognize, however, is the fact that the pool itself would not exist were it not for those who have purchased policies from the insurer. The existence of that pool enables every insured to have its risk spread among all of the participants. The parent's situation is no different.[794]

In denying the deduction for a captive that has non-parent risk, the service is relying on its argument from *Carnation* and *Clougherty*: when the captive makes a payment to the parent, the captive's stock price decreases. This in turn lowers the value of the parent's assets. However, when the captive insures a large enough pool of non-parent risk, payment of the parent's claim is taken from a large enough pool of risk that the payment does not decrease the captive's stock price—at least not significantly enough to negatively impact the parent's balance sheet values.

**Malone and Hyde**

*Malone and Hyde* is an interesting case because the *Humana* decision occurred right at the end of the original trial. As a result, the petitioner filed a motion "for reconsideration … and to supplement facts."[795] The court granted this motion and re-decided the brother-sister issue in favor of the petitioner. In addition, on rehearing, the court applied the three-prong test established in *Harper*.

---

794   *Id.* at 167.
795   Malone and Hyde, Inc. and Subsidiaries v. C.I.R., T.C. Memo 1993-585, section 2.

For the years in question (1978–1980), Malone and Hyde was a publicly traded company with subsidiaries in retail food, auto parts, drugstore, insurance, and financial services.[796] Starting in the mid-1970s, Malone and Hyde began looking into alternate insurance possibilities because of the structure of its insurance policies with CNA.[797] Malone and Hyde[798] hired Risk Management, Inc. (RMI) to advise them on the possibility of establishing a captive insurance company.[799] RMI proposed a two-step plan, with the first step involving the creation of the captive, which would only insure Malone and Hyde and its subsidiaries, while the second stage would involve the insurance of non–Malone and Hyde businesses (if stage one proved successful).[800] Malone and Hyde incorporated Eastland Insurance on June 21, 1977, in Bermuda.[801] The captive issued 120,000 shares at one dollar per share, all of which were purchased by Malone and Hyde.[802] Malone hired an RMI management subsidiary to run the captive.[803]

Malone and Hyde used Eastland to reinsure the first $150,000 of coverage under a new insurance agreement with Northwestern National Insurance Company.[804] Under the terms of the insurance agreement, Malone and Hyde paid Northwestern, who in turn ceded a percentage of the payment received to

---

796 *Malone and Hyde*, T.C. Memo 1989-604.
797 *Id.*
798 *Id.*
799 *Id.*
800 *Id.*
801 *Id.*
802 *Id.*
803 *Id.*
804 *Id.*

Eastland.[805] Eastland in turn issued an irrevocable letter of credit to Northwestern in the amount of $250,000.[806] In addition, Malone and Hyde signed a hold harmless agreement with Northwestern.[807]

Eastland operated as a standard property and casualty insurer.[808] For the first year in question (1979), Eastland received reinsurance premiums from Northwestern in the amount of $2,002,393, while in 1980, Eastland received $2,367,321 in reinsurance premiums.[809]

At trial, the petitioner did not raise the brother-sister issue.[810] Therefore, the court originally dealt with only the parent-captive issue.[811] As such, the holdings in *Carnation* and *Clougherty* were still determinative, leading the court to rule against the petitioner.[812]

There were important changes to the court's analysis on repetition. First, in the factual recitation, the court spent more time discussing the actual inner workings of Eastland's insurance methodology—how it was paid, how it determined premiums, and how the parent allocated the insurance premiums among the various subsidiaries. In the previous decision, this was not

---

805   *Id.*
806   *Id.*
807   *Id.*
808   *Id.* Eastland established loss reserves, case reserves, but not reported reserves. In addition, the Eastland paid claims out of an individual bank account.
809   *Id.*
810   *Id.*
811   *Id.*
812   *Id.*

necessary, because the court was not deciding the brother-sister issue, and the parent-captive issue was governed completely by *Carnation* and *Clougherty*. However, between the initial case and the re-determination, the tax court issued *Harper*, which had a new three-prong test.[813] As such, the analysis of the situation had changed.

The tax court first concluded that Malone and Hyde faced insurance risks: "In this case, the various subsidiaries of Malone & Hyde faced substantial potential workers' compensation, automobile, and general liability risks."[814]

Next, the court ruled risk shifting did occur.[815] The court again used the "balance sheet test," where the central issue is whether the insured owns stock in the insurance company.[816] If so, then a payment from the captive will lower its stock price, which will in turn lower the insured's total assets, making the payment look more like self-insurance than actual insurance.[817] The court noted,

> As the Sixth Circuit observed, the economic reality of insurance between subsidiaries and a captive insurance company, where the subsidiaries own no stock in the captive and vice versa, is one in which the subsidiaries'

---

[813] *Harper*, 96. T.C. 45, 58: "whether the arrangement involves the existence of insurance risk, whether there was risk shifting and risk distribution and whether the arrangement was for 'insurance' in the commonly accepted sense."

[814] *Malone and Hyde, Inc. and Subsidiaries v. C.I.R.*, T.C. Memo 1993-585 section 10.

[815] *Id.* at section 11.

[816] *Id.* at section 10.

[817] *Id.* at section 11.

balance sheets and net worth are not adversely affected when a loss is sustained by a subsidiary and payment is made by the captive insurance subsidiary.[818]

In this case, Malone and Hyde's subsidiaries owned no stock in the captive insurance company. Therefore, a payment from the captive to the subsidiary would not lower the subsidiaries' total assets. Hence, there was risk shifting.[819]

On re-determination, the service argued that Malone and Hyde's hold harmless agreement and Eastland's irrevocable letter of credit to Northwestern prevented the policies from being insurance.[820] However, the court dismissed this argument, noting,

> The subsidiaries were not parties to the Hold Harmless Agreement between Malone & Hyde and Northwestern or the letters of credit between Eastland and Northwestern. They did not agree in any way to contribute to Eastland's capital or to pay any losses should Eastland be unable to perform its obligations. From the subsidiaries' perspective, the Hold Harmless Agreement and letters of credit merely provided additional assurance that their insured losses would be paid and that they would not have to bear their own losses. Their financial obligations regarding claims for losses ended with payment of their allocated shares of the premium.[821]

---

818 *Id.*
819 *Id.*
820 *Id.*
821 *Id.*

Eastland signed the irrevocable letter of credit and sent it to Northwestern. In the event Eastland would have to pay under the letter of credit, the payment would move from Eastland to Northwestern. This would not affect the balance sheet of any subsidiary. In addition, Malone and Hyde's hold harmless agreement was between Malone and Hyde and Northwestern; the agreement had no bearing on the captives. In short, "[the subsidiaries] did not agree in any way to contribute to Eastland's capital or to pay any losses should Eastland be unable to perform its obligations."[822] In addition, the service also argued that the presence of the letter of credit and hold harmless agreement indicated the insurance contracts were not bona fide, because neither contract would be necessary if the insurance contracts were legitimate.[823] However, the court merely found both to be prudent business decisions on the part of Northwestern.[824]

The court next ruled that Eastland was a bona fide insurance company. Eastland was not a sham, nor did it lack a legitimate business purpose. Therefore, the court could not use a "substance over form" argument to rule the company invalid.[825] Eastland was

> adequately capitalized according to Bermuda's insurance law. The record establishes that Eastland was formed for legitimate business purposes. We have found that Eastland operated in the same manner as other insurance companies. It established reserve

---

822 *Id.*
823 *Id.* at 12.
824 *Id.*
825 *Id.* at 13.

accounts, paid claimed losses only after the validity of those claims had been established, and was profitable, much in accordance with industry standards. The policies into which it entered were valid and binding. All of these factors cumulatively indicate that Eastland was a valid insurance company.[826]

Notice the court is focusing on how the insurance company was run. In essence, if the company looks and acts like an insurance company, the court is required to respect the company's existence as required by *Moline Properties*.

Finally, the court ruled there was risk distribution.[827] The court noted that risk distribution must accomplish one of the following:

> (1) spreading losses among insureds; (2) providing an insurance company with a pool of premiums from which to pay losses; and (3) serving as a prerequisite to the application of the "law of large numbers."[828]

The service argued there was an insufficient number of subsidiaries for risk distribution to exist.[829] The court ruled that eight subsidiaries were sufficient.[830] However, the court also noted that Eastland provided

---

826  *Id.*
827  *Id.* at 14.
828  *Id.*
829  *Id.*
830  *Id.*

workers' compensation coverage for 6,700 to 7,100 employees of Malone & Hyde, its subsidiaries and divisions; automobile liability coverage for 1,800 automobiles, trucks, and trailers; and general liability coverage for most of petitioner's warehouses and retail stores. Commentators have noted that "when an insurer has a sufficiently large number of risks such that great variations in aggregate losses are unlikely, and the premiums received plus its capital make it a viable risk bearer, one can say that risk distribution is present regardless of the number of insureds covered."[831]

In other words, the large number of different insurance policies played some role in the court's determination.

**Kidde**

*Kidde* is important because the service would attempt to use a new argument to thwart a captive insurance program. The service would argue that a corporation was in fact a "nexus of contracts"; therefore, the case analysis required the court to look at the effect of the transaction on each shareholder.

"Kidde was a broad-based, decentralized conglomerate with approximately 15 separate operating divisions and 100 wholly owned subsidiaries, each of which Kidde treated as an independent profit center."[832] In 1976, the company could not obtain product liability insurance at an attractive rate.[833] As a result, third-

---

831 *Id.*
832 *Kidde*, 40 Fed. Cl. 42, 44.
833 *Id.* at 45.

party insurers required Kidde to start a captive insurance company that would reinsure the third-party insurers.[834] Kidde started the Kidde Insurance Company (KIC) in Bermuda on December 22, 1976, with $1 million in initial capital.[835] Kidde purchased insurance from two AIG affiliates (National Union Fire Insurance Company and American Home Assurance Company), who in turn ceded a portion of the payment in the form of a reinsurance policy payment to KIC.[836] KIC assumed the first $1 million of each workers' compensation claim and the first $2.5 million of each products liability claim.[837] For the years 1977 and 1978, Kidde deducted the entire payment made to third-party insurers.[838] The IRS disallowed the amount of the deductions that eventually went to KIC.[839]

The court began its analysis of the deductibility of the insurance payments by first asking whether or not the arrangement was a sham.[840] Although this actual description has not been used in a previous case, it is consistent with the application of *Moline Properties* to any captive insurance facts. If the captive is not a sham, then *Moline Properties* requires the court to treat the captive as a separate legal entity.[841] In addition, this analysis

---

834  *Id.*
835  *Id.*
836  *Id.*
837  *Id.*
838  *Id.* at 46.
839  *Id.*
840  *Id.* at 50.
841  See *Moline Properties*, 438-39: "The doctrine of corporate entity fills a useful purpose in business life. Whether the purpose be to gain an advantage under the law of the state of incorporation or to avoid or to comply with the demands of creditors or to serve the creator's personal or undisclosed convenience, so long as that purpose is the equivalent of business activity or is followed by the carrying on

is consistent with factor number 3 from *Harper*—whether the arrangement was for "insurance" in its commonly accepted sense.[842] A commonly accepted notion of insurance would not involve a transaction with a sham corporation.

The court ruled that KIC was not a sham for three reasons. First, Kidde could have self-insured, but in order to do so, it would have had to set up a program in over forty states in order to comply with forty different state insurance regulators.[843] A captive insurance company eliminated this problem. Second, using a third-party insurer (which in turn purchased a reinsurance policy from KIC) allowed Kidde to "maintain existing prices and policies for catastrophic insurance."[844] Third, Kidde eventually wanted KIC to insure non-Kidde risks and thereby become a separate profit center for the company.[845] Individually, any one of these facts would trump an argument that the captive was a sham. Combined, they are that much more persuasive.

The court next analyzed whether or not the policy was insurance.[846] This analysis corresponds to the third prong of the *Harper* test—whether the arrangement was for insurance in its commonly accepted sense.[847] The court looked at the policies from an intra-company perspective and found them adequate. Each company that purchased a policy (Kidde from

---

    of business by the corporation, the corporation remains a separate taxable entity."
842  *Harper*, 96 T.C. 45, 58.
843  *Kidde*, 40 Fed. Cl. at 51.
844  *Id.*
845  *Id.*
846  *Id.*
847  *Harper*, 96 T.C. 45, 58.

National and National from KIC) paid a premium in return for the other party's assuming a certain risk of the purchaser.[848] In addition, third parties who filed a claim against Kidde "interacted with KIC representatives in essentially the same way as claimants interact with representatives of any other reinsurance company."[849]

The commissioner advanced three arguments against the conclusion that the arrangement between the companies was insurance in its commonly held sense. First, KIC's incorporation in Bermuda raised suspicions on the transaction because Bermuda had less regulation.[850] However, the court ruled that a corporation can choose to locate its operations in a location that will result in "maximum profits for the corporation."[851] Next, the service argued that Kidde exercised too much control of KIC,[852] essentially arguing KIC was Kidde's alter-ego and should therefore be disregarded. The court overruled this argument. In staffing KIC with Kidde employees, "Kidde not only wanted to take advantage of the expertise of its own employees in overseeing KIC's operation but also wanted to keep firm control over KIC's day-to-day operations."[853] Finally, the service argued that

> KIC was virtually an invisible company which existed primarily on paper. KIC had minimal contacts in Bermuda. It had no employees and no separate offices

---

848 *Kidde*, 40 Fed. Cl. at 51-52.
849 *Id.* at 52.
850 *Id.*
851 *Id.*
852 *Id.*
853 *Id.* at 52.

in Bermuda and operated in Bermuda through a management company specializing in managing captive insurance companies. The management company prepared a limited amount of documents annually for KIC. KIC contracted with third parties, primarily companies related to AIG, for most of the typical functions performed by insurance companies, including, as noted above, the processing of insurance claims.[854]

However, the court noted that although Bermudan business practices were different from US corporate practices, this was not enough of a reason to render the transactions void.[855] In short, the court endorsed the idea of offshore insurance with this part of its ruling.

However, the most important point of *Kidde* is the service's new anti-captive argument. The service now proffered a new expert—Dr. Gregory Niehaus—who offered the following analysis:

> [M]odern economic theory views a corporation as a nexus of contracts among individual stakeholders and evaluates corporate decisions based on how the individual stakeholders are affected. Consistent with this approach, Professor Niehaus argued that corporations do not bear risk but rather individual stakeholders bear risk. Hence, defendant argues, in determining whether risk shifting or risk distributing occurred herein, the court should focus on the individual shareholders of Kidde, and the risk faced by

---

854  *Id.*
855  *Id.*

these shareholders is not affected when one subsidiary assumes legal responsibility for the claims against the other subsidiaries.[856]

In essence, the modern corporation is really a collection of shareholders who pool their interests in a corporate form. To analyze a transaction requires an analysis of how the transaction affects each individual shareholder. In effect, this theory treats a corporation as a partnership. While the court agreed with this analysis,[857] it also stated that this theory runs straight into *Moline Properties* and general tax law concepts, which require the court to look at each company as a separate legal entity. As such, the payments from the subsidiaries are deductible because the subsidiaries have no ownership interest in the captive.[858] In addition, the subsidiary is transferring its risk into a large enough pool of risk that risk distribution occurs.[859]

Regarding the insurance payments from the parent to the subsidiary, the court would eventually rule that because the captive did not insure non-Kidde companies for the years in question, no risk distribution occurred (and therefore, the payments from the parent to the captive were non-deductible).[860] However, the court arrived at this decision in a slightly different way then the "balance sheet" argument of *Carnation* and *Clougherty*. First, the plaintiff argued the court should allow the parent to deduct its premium to the captive because the captive did in fact have sufficient risk

---

856   *Id.* at 55.
857   *Id.*
858   *Id.*
859   *Id.*
860   *Id.* at 57-58.

distribution—even if the risk distribution occurred because of insurance provided to the parent's subsidiaries.[861] The court did not agree, first noting that the parent must transfer not only "risk" but the "variability of loss," i.e. "the risk that the amount of the loss suffered will exceed the average or expected amount of loss."[862] In effect, the purpose of insurance is to stick the insurance company with the bigger bill. Therefore, there are in fact two kinds of risk:

> the level of risk transferred to the captive insurer and the level of risk ultimately shouldered by the parent. If the risk ultimately shouldered by the parent is less than the risk transferred, then the required risk shifting occurred. If the two levels of risk are the same, however, then no risk shifting occurred even though the captive insurer has become legally responsible for the parent's claims.[863]

When the parent owns the captive and the captive only insures the parent and the parent's subsidiaries, the parent does not lower its risk below the amount of risk transferred to the captive. For example, if a parent company owns all the stock of the captive and the captive pays $1,000 to the parent for an insurance claim, the captive's stock will drop by $1,000. However, suppose the captive insures another independent company's risk. Now when the captive pays the parent, the captive's stock price does not decrease nearly as much. This is because the law of large numbers has started

---

861 *Id.* at 56.
862 *Id.* at 57.
863 *Id.*

to take hold and the amount of the loss expectation and experience approaches one.

> The question then becomes how this unrelated business operates to change the variability of loss faced by the parent. The Federal Circuit's answer appears to lie in the parent, through the arrangement involving the captive insurer, placing the risks faced by the parent into a pool with other independently insured risks. As explained above pursuant to the law of large numbers, the variability of loss decreases when risks are combined with other independent risks. Hence, from the parent's perspective, when risks faced by the parent become the responsibility of a wholly owned subsidiary, and the subsidiary in turn combines those risks with other independent risks of corporations unrelated to the parent, the net effect is that the parent will shoulder less risk because it has a lower variability of loss than it faced before it entered the arrangement with its subsidiary.[864]

However,

> [t]here is no analogous decrease in risk where, as in the instant case, the risk combined by the captive insurer involved essentially only future claims against the parent and its wholly owned subsidiaries. Because the parent owns the subsidiary corporations, its net assets, as reflected on its balance sheet, would decrease

---

864   *Id.* at 75.

dollar for dollar with any loss suffered by any one of those subsidiaries.[865]

Finally, the plaintiff offered two more arguments, which the court quickly dismissed. First, the plaintiff argued risk shifting occurred because Kidde paid National and then National paid KIC.[866] However, National would not agree to insure Kidde unless Kidde provided some form of reinsurance.[867] In effect, "from the beginning, the parties understood that KIC rather than National would be responsible for these claims, and that Kidde's payments relating to such coverage would be ceded to KIC."[868] In short, because the payments were always destined for the captive, the payment to the third party was not legally meaningful. Finally, the plaintiff argued that because Kidde intended to seek non-Kidde business from 1980 onward, the court should allow deductions for claims that had been filed but not paid.[869] However, the plaintiff did not offer any evidence of the value of these claims.[870]

## UPS

*UPS* represents the service's Hail Mary attempt to stop the use of captive insurance. Until this point, the courts had completely rejected the "economic family" doctrine that formed the basis of the service's anti-captive argument. Next, the service attempted to argue that a corporation was in fact a nexus of

---

865 *Id.*
866 *Id.* at 58.
867 *Id.*
868 *Id.*
869 *Id.* at 59.
870 *Id.*

contracts. Therefore, the court should analyze the insurance transaction to determine its effect on each shareholder. Now, the service simply argued a transaction involving a captive insurer was in fact an assignment-of-income case.

United Parcel Service (UPS) charged its clients an extra fee to insure packages above one hundred dollars in value.[871] This was income to UPS.[872] UPS's insurance broker suggested UPS restructure this transaction to avoid the addition to UPS's gross income of excess value charges (EVCs).[873] UPS implemented this plan by forming a Bermudan captive named Overseas Partners (OPL) in 1983.[874] UPS then purchased an insurance policy from National Union Fire Insurance Company (NUF), who in turn purchased reinsurance from OPL.[875] As a result, the payment from UPS to NUF would be classified as an insurance premium and therefore deductible under 26 U.S.C. 162(a).

The IRS attacked this arrangement, arguing "that the excess-value payment remitted ultimately to OPL had to be treated as gross income to UPS."[876] In effect, the IRS was now making an assignment-of-income argument in an attempt to thwart UPS's captive arrangement.[877] There were two reasons for this change of tactic. First, the IRS's previous arguments were not successful; no court had accepted the "economic family" doctrine, and after the court in *Humana* rejected that

---

871 *United Parcel Service*, 254 F.3d 1014, 1016.
872 See 26 U.S.C. 61(a): "Except as otherwise provided in this subtitle, gross income means all income from whatever source derived."
873 *United Parcel Service*, 254 F.3d at 1016.
874 *Id.*
875 *Id.*
876 *Id.* at 1017.
877 *United Parcel Service*, T.C. Memo 1999-268, section 21.

argument, the service made a new and unsuccessful use of the argument that corporations are a series of contracts. Second, the assignment of income doctrine avoided having to work around the separate corporate entity issue of the captive that had plagued previous captive cases.[878]

In analyzing UPS's situation before and after it established the captive, the tax court noted that UPS performed all the work related to the EVCs before and after the transaction:[879]

> Before January 1, 1984, petitioner performed all the functions and activities related to the EVCs and was liable for the damage or loss of packages up to their declared value. After January 1, 1984, petitioner continued to perform all the functions and activities related to EVC's, including billing for and receiving EVC's, and remained liable to shippers whose shipments were damaged or lost while in petitioner's possession. Petitioner continued to receive shippers' claims for lost or damaged goods, investigate and adjust such claims, and pay such claims out of the EVC revenue that it had collected from shippers. The difference between petitioner's EVC activity before and after January 1, 1984 was that after that date it

---

878  *Id.* "Respondent does not, and need not, challenge OPL's separate existence as a valid corporate entity. The classic assignment of income cases involve persons and entities whose separate existence was unquestioned. See *United States v. Basve, supra; Lucas v. Earl, supra; Leavell v. Commissioner*, 104 T.C. 140 (1995). The Supreme Court's articulation of the assignment of income doctrine requires no challenge to the separate existence of the persons or entities to which the doctrine applies."

879  *Id.* at section 22 and section 23.

remitted the excess of EVC revenues over claims paid, i.e. gross profit, to NUF, which, after subtracting relatively small fronting fees and expenses, paid the remainder to OPL, which was essentially owned by petitioner's shareholders.[880]

The only difference between UPS's pre- and post-1984 arrangements was the insertion of NUF and OPL into the equation.[881] However, if that arrangement did not have economic substance, the court would not recognize the arrangement.[882] Hence, at trial, this case's focus was the objective and subjective substance of the transactions between UPS and NUF, and NUF and OPL.[883]

UPS first stated it created the transaction between UPS, NUF, and OPL out of concern that the EVCs were insurance for which UPS did not have the requisite state licenses.[884] As a result, UPS's business purpose for the transaction was to bring an existing business practice in line with various state laws. However, for this claim to be valid, UPS would have to demonstrate that it "was motivated by a good faith concern that it was illegal for petitioner to continue to receive the excess value income."[885] But UPS never obtained a legal opinion regarding the possible legal status of the EVC program.[886][887]

---

880  *Id.* at section 23.
881  *Id.* at section 24.
882  *Id.*
883  *Id.*
884  *Id.* at 25.
885  *Id.*
886  *Id.* at 26.
887  See also sections 29 and 30: Petitioner's assertion that it was concerned about state insurance regulation was proved inaccurate

In addition, after the program was in place, UPS continued to sell EVC policies to shippers in the same manner as before the transaction was established.[888] Finally, at trial, UPS did not offer any documentary evidence to back up this assertion.[889]

Others of petitioner's arguments were proven inaccurate by documentary evidence or testimony at trial. First, UPS argued that its business purpose for establishing OPL was to create a viable insurance company as a profit center for the company overall.[890] However, the court noted that there were plenty of ways UPS could capitalize this new venture without diverting excess value premiums to OPL. UPS also argued its business purpose was to allow the company to raise insurance rates.[891] But this assertion was proven incorrect by testimony from the petitioner's own witness at trial.[892] UPS also argued the new arrangement was a form of asset protection—that it lowered UPS's exposure to risk and therefore protected the company's core assets.[893] However, UPS continued to be primarily liable on many aspects of the EVCs after the implementation of the captive insurance company.[894] Therefore, the company was still essentially liable, and its claim was proven incorrect by the facts.

---

by the plaintiff's own assertion of federal law related to common carrier regulation under the Carmack Amendment in previous cases involving petitioner. In short, petitioner's previous actions proved this assertion as wrong.
888   *Id.* at 27.
889   *Id.* at 25.
890   *Id.* at section 30.
891   *Id.*
892   *Id.* at 31.
893   *Id.*
894   *Id.* at 31-32.

The court next determined whether the rate charged by UPS for its EVC policy was an arm's-length price. The service procured an expert named Mr. Kelly to demonstrate that the rates charged for EVCs were higher than would be charged in a competitive market.[895] To demonstrate this fact, Mr. Kelly noted that OPL had a loss ratio of 33 percent—meaning the company paid out approximately 33 percent of premiums received in the form of payment for claims.[896] Mr. Kelly testified that this rate of profit retention would have driven clients away.[897] The court also noted that another UPS subsidiary named PIP charged a lower rate (0.125 cents per one hundred dollars—about half the EVC rate) for its insurance.[898] Several other experts backed up this claim. Even an expert procured by the petitioner conceded that UPS's EVC rates were high.[899] As such, the court determined that the rates charged were not at arm's length, making the transaction a sham for tax purposes.[900]

Finally, the court noted that the petitioner's sole purpose for entering into the transaction was lowering its federal tax burden.[901] The petitioner's insurance broker prepared an original report stating that UPS could save $16 million in federal taxes the first year the plan was put in effect.[902] Other documents procured at trial demonstrated that tax reasons were the petitioner's primary motivation for entering into the transaction.[903]

---

895 *Id.* 34.
896 *Id.*
897 *Id.*
898 *Id.*
899 *Id.* at 36-37.
900 *Id.* at 37.
901 *Id.*
902 *Id.* at 38.
903 *Id.*

For all of the reasons listed, the court ruled that the payments UPS deducted as insurance premiums were not legitimate business deductions.[904] UPS appealed the decision.[905]

After mentioning the general facts, the appellate court first noted, "It is not perfectly clear on what judicial doctrine the holding rests."[906] Next, the court noted that this was essentially a sham transaction case, with the IRS arguing that the court should not respect the transaction because its only motive was tax avoidance.[907] The court first outlined the basic concept of the sham transaction doctrine:

> This economic-substance doctrine, also called the sham-transaction doctrine, provides that a transaction ceases to merit tax respect when it has no "economic effects other than the creation of tax benefits." Even if the transaction has economic effects, it must be disregarded if it has no business purpose and its motive is tax avoidance.[908]

In other words, the plaintiff must prove that there is a legitimate, non-tax business purpose to the transaction in order to avoid the application of the sham-transaction doctrine.

The appellate court noted that "economic effects" include the creation of genuine obligations enforceable by an unrelated

---

904  *Id.* at 39.
905  *Id.*
906  *United Parcel Service*, 254 F.3d 1014.
907  *Id.* at 1017.
908  *Id.* at 1018.

party.⁹⁰⁹ The court noted that a legitimate insurance contract existed between OPL and NUL, which NUL had the right to enforce.⁹¹⁰ The tax court "dismissed these obligations" because of the reinsurance agreement between NUL and OPL, arguing that NUL was nothing more than a conduit for payment from UPS to OPL.⁹¹¹ In addition, UPS actually lost the income, given OPL's separate taxable status.⁹¹² Finally, the court noted that the tax court was stretching the business purpose doctrine farther than it was intended to go.⁹¹³ The court sided with UPS and remanded the case back to the trial level.⁹¹⁴

UPS's case at trial was poorly presented. Despite UPS being a large, multi-national corporation with a legal department to match, it offered no evidence of legitimate business reasons for entering into the OPL transaction. It is hard to imagine none existed, especially when UPS's tax attorney restructured the originally proposed transaction to take the Bermuda company out of the controlled foreign corporation section of the tax code.⁹¹⁵ This indicates a high degree of sophistication, which would not be tripped up by an inability to demonstrate a legitimate business purpose for the transaction. Simply put, the trial attorneys appear to have been caught flatfooted. In addition, there was no mention of the factors from *Harper*. Had the petitioner simply used the *Harper* factors as a roadmap to prove that OPL was a legitimate captive, there would have

---

909  *Id.*
910  *Id.*
911  *Id.* at 1019.
912  *Id.*
913  *Id.*
914  *Id.* at 102.
915  *United Parcel Service* at section 8.

been no problem. Finally, *Harper* also involved an international shipping company that won against an IRS challenge. The fact that a company in the same line of business lost is ridiculous.

In addition, the appellate opinion is rather weak. While the case will have some procedural weight simply because of who wrote it (a federal appellate court), I would be uncomfortable using this specific case as an example of brilliant legal reasoning—especially relating to the sham transaction or business purpose doctrine. My guess is that the court is simply looking for a reason—any reason—to end this specific litigation and captive litigation in general. By the time of this decision, the government had been losing captive cases for over ten years. The writing was on the wall: in certain situations, the courts would find captives to be legitimate business planning tools. No court had ever adopted the IRS's central reasoning (the "economic family" doctrine) for challenging captives. This was the second case when the IRS had changed its legal theory regarding captives with similar results—a loss. In short, the court is saying, "No matter how you challenge a captive, we're probably going to rule against the service."

**Revenue Ruling 2002-89**

By the beginning of the 2000s, it was obvious that courts would accept captive insurance. Therefore, the IRS shifted its tactics. Instead of challenging captives at every turn, the IRS would now provide some guidance regarding these structures, while still reserving the right to challenge transactions it thought were abusive. This practice began with Revenue Ruling 2001-31, where the IRS first acknowledged that no court had fully accepted the "economic family" theory first advanced in Revenue Ruling 77-316.[916] As a result, the service was abandoning that theory with regard to captive insurance companies.[917] However, the service would still challenge certain transactions based on individual facts and circumstances.[918] In essence, the service put to rest its primary theory for challenging captive insurance companies.

But the service would go further. In Revenue Ruling 2002-89, the service outlined two different fact scenarios in order to endorse a specific method of arranging a captive's business:

> Situation 1. P, a domestic corporation, enters into an annual arrangement with its wholly owned domestic subsidiary, S, whereby S "insures" the professional liability risks of P either directly or as a reinsurer of these risks. S is regulated as an insurance company in each state where S does business.
>
> The amounts P pays to S under the arrangement are established according to customary industry rating formulas. In all respects, the parties conduct themselves consistently with the standards applicable to an insurance arrangement between unrelated parties.
>
> In implementing the arrangement, S may perform all necessary administrative tasks, or it may outsource those tasks at prevailing commercial market rates. P

---

916   Rev. Rul. 2001-31.
917   *Id.*
918   *Id.*

does not provide any guarantee of S's performance, and all funds and business records of P and S are separately maintained. S does not loan any funds to P.

In addition to the arrangement with P, S enters into insurance contracts whereby S serves as a direct insurer or a reinsurer of the professional liability risks of entities unrelated to P or S. The risks of unrelated entities and those of P are homogeneous. The amounts S receives from these unrelated entities under these insurance contracts likewise are established according to customary industry rating formulas.

The premiums S earns from the arrangement with P constitute 90% of S's total premiums earned during the taxable year on both a gross and net basis. The liability coverage S provides to P accounts for 90% of the total risks borne by S.

Situation 2. Situation 2 is the same as Situation 1 except that the premiums S earns from the arrangement with P constitute less than 50% of S's total premiums earned during the taxable year on both a gross and net basis. The liability coverage S provides to P accounts for less than 50% of the total risks borne by S.[919]

The first three paragraphs are a tacit admission of two of three of the *Harper* three-prong analysis. The fact that the parent needs professional liability insurance demonstrates the "existence of

---

919   Rev. Rul. 2002-89.

insurance risk."[920] All the services that the captive will provide, as well as the captive's method of doing business—arm's-length pricing and the captive's ability to stand on its own and perform all the services expected of a captive—demonstrate the arrangement "was for 'insurance' in its commonly accepted sense."[921] The only difference between the scenarios is the percentage of outside business the captive underwrites. In the first scenario, the captive has 10 percent exposure to non-parent insurance business, while in the second scenario, the captive has 50 percent exposure to non-parent business. According to this revenue ruling, the first scenario does not have sufficient non-parent exposure to be considered a legitimate insurance company. The reason is that the first scenario does not have sufficient risk distribution (the amount of non-parent risk the captive takes on), while the second situation has sufficient risk distribution. Therefore, the service is also accepting the second (and final) prong of the *Harper* decision—whether there was both risk shifting and risk distribution.[922] In other words, this ruling stands for the proposition that the IRS will not challenge a captive insurance company's tax status—and will therefore allow the parent to deduct full insurance premiums—if the captive underwrites at least 50 percent of its business with a non-parent insured. However, the *Harper* decision also contained this fact, which contradicts the service's position: "Here, the relatively large number of unrelated insureds comprise approximately 30% of [the captive's] business; such a level of unrelated insureds, in our opinion, constitutes a sufficient pool of insureds to provide risk distribution."[923]

---

920 *Harper*, 96 T.C. 45, 58.
921 *Id.*
922 *Harper*, 96 T.C. at 58.
923 *Id.* at 59-60.

**Revenue Ruling 2002-90**

In its next revenue ruling, the IRS would expand on its thinking regarding captive insurance companies:

> P, a domestic holding company, owns all of the stock of 12 domestic subsidiaries that provide professional services. Each subsidiary in the P group has a geographic territory comprised of a state in which the subsidiary provides professional services. The subsidiaries in the P group operate on a decentralized basis. The services provided by the employees of each subsidiary are performed under the general guidance of a supervisory professional for a particular facility of the subsidiary. The general categories of the professional services rendered by each of the subsidiaries are the same throughout the P group. Together the 12 subsidiaries have a significant volume of independent, homogeneous risks.
>
> P, for a valid non-tax business purpose, forms S as a wholly-owned insurance subsidiary under the laws of State C. P provides S adequate capital and S is fully licensed in State C and in the 11 other states where the respective operating subsidiaries conduct their professional service businesses. S directly insures the professional liability risks of the 12 operating subsidiaries in the P group. S charges the 12 subsidiaries arms-length premiums, which are established according to customary industry rating formulas. None of the operating subsidiaries have

liability coverage for less than 5%, nor more than 15%, of the total risk insured by S. S retains the risks that it insures from the 12 operating subsidiaries. There are no parental (or other related party) guarantees of any kind made in favor of S. S does not loan any funds to P or to the 12 operating subsidiaries. In all respects, the parties conduct themselves in a manner consistent with the standards applicable to an insurance arrangement between unrelated parties. S does not provide coverage to any entity other than the 12 operating subsidiaries.[924]

Notice that the above scenario outlines a situation similar to that of *Humana*, where a parent corporation owns all the stock of a group of subsidiaries.[925] The subsidiaries were formed for legitimate business reasons—namely, dividing the country into geographically separate units and then assigning each "division" a unique territory. In addition, each division could essentially stand on its own as an independent business. Finally, each subsidiary faces legitimate risk in the conduct of its business. Simply put, this fact pattern avoids the allegation that the subsidiaries were not formed for a legitimate business purpose and should therefore be disregarded.[926]

The parent forms a subsidiary that is a captive insurance company. The captive operates as an independent entity; it charges commercially determined rates, it is fully licensed, and

---

[924] Rev. Rul. 2002-90.
[925] See *Humana*, 881 F.2d 247.
[926] *Black's Law Dictionary*: "The principle that a transaction must serve a bona fide business purpose (i.e. not just for tax avoidance) to qualify for beneficial tax treatment."

it is adequately capitalized.[927] In other words, the transaction complies with two to the three prongs outlined in *Harper*.[928] As a result, the IRS determined the above scenario was insurance for tax purposes.[929] Note that no single company comprises more than 15 percent of the total insurance risk borne by the captive. This is a key takeaway from this revenue ruling: when a captive insures a group of subsidiaries and no subsidiary comprises more than 15 percent of the total risk of the captive, the IRS will recognize the transaction as insurance for federal tax purposes.

In addition, the number of subsidiaries in this example is important, sometimes referred to as the "rule of twelve." That is, when the parent has at least twelve subsidiaries, the IRS will not challenge the transaction.[930]

**Revenue Ruling 2002-91**

Next, the IRS would issue 2002-91, which offered the following fact pattern:

> X is one of a small group of unrelated businesses involved in one highly concentrated industry. Businesses involved in this industry face significant liability hazards. X and the other businesses involved in this industry are required by regulators to maintain adequate liability insurance coverage in order to

---

[927] Rev. Rul. 2002-90.
[928] *Harper*, 96 T.C. 45, 58: "(1) whether the arrangement involves the existence of an 'insurance risk'; (2) whether there was both risk shifting and risk distribution; and, (3) whether the arrangement was for 'insurance' in its commonly accepted sense."
[929] *Id.*
[930] Wright, Weber, and Lynch, *Seeking Out Safe Harbors*.

continue to operate. Businesses that participate in this industry have sustained significant losses due to the occurrence of unusually severe loss events. As a result, affordable insurance coverage for businesses that participate in this industry is not available from commercial insurance companies.

X and a significant number of the businesses involved in this industry (Members) form a so-called "group captive" (GC) to provide insurance coverage for stated liability risks. GC provides insurance only to X and the other Members. The business operations of GC are separate from the business operation of each Member. GC is adequately capitalized.

No Member owns more than 15% of GC, and no Member has more than 15% of the vote on any corporate governance issue. In addition, no Member's individual risk insured by GC exceeds 15% of the total risk insured by GC. Thus, no one member controls GC.

GC issues insurance contracts and charges premiums for the insurance coverage provided under the contracts. GC uses recognized actuarial techniques, based, in part, on commercial rates for similar coverage, to determine the premiums to be charged to an individual Member.

GC pools all the premiums it receives in its general funds and pays claims out of those funds. GC investigates any claim made by a Member to determine the validity of the claim prior to making any payment on that claim. GC conducts no other business than the issuing and administering of insurance contracts.

No Member has any obligation to pay GC additional premiums if that Member's actual losses during any period of coverage exceed the premiums paid by that Member. No Member will be entitled to a refund of premiums paid if that Member's actual losses are lower than the premiums paid for coverage during any period. Premiums paid by any Member may be used to satisfy claims of the other Members. No Member that terminates its insurance coverage or sells its ownership interest in GC is required to make additional premium or capital payments to GC to cover losses in excess of its premiums paid. Moreover, no Member that terminates its coverage or disposes of its ownership interest in GC is entitled to a refund of premiums paid in excess of insured losses.[931]

The companies in this revenue ruling have a high-risk exposure and are required to maintain insurance that the market is not providing—also a common fact pattern in the captive cases. Like the preceding two revenue rulings, the companies here formed the captive for legitimate business reasons, complying with two of the three prongs outlined in *Harper*:[932] no company has control; the insureds face true hazards; and insurance rates

---

931 Rev. Rul. 2002-91.
932 *Harper*, 96 T.C. 45, 58: "(1) whether the arrangement involves the existence of an 'insurance risk,' ... (3) whether the arrangement was for 'insurance' in its commonly accepted sense."

are determined according to industry convention and at market-determined prices. The captive was adequately capitalized and was a separate entity from the other companies. Additionally, assuming the articles of incorporation use standard majority rule, it would take four members to form a simple majority (totaling 55 percent) and five to form a super majority (75 percent). In addition—like the fact pattern in the preceding revenue ruling—no company accounts for more than 15 percent of the total risk insured by the captive,[933] indicating that there is sufficient risk distribution.[934] This revenue ruling is the exact same structure approved by the court in *Humana*.

In addition, some commentators have suggested that this revenue ruling lowers the safe harbor rule of twelve down to seven.[935]

**Revenue Ruling 2005-40**

Finally, for our purposes, the IRS issued Revenue Ruling 2005-40, which offered four different fact patterns:

> Situation 1. X, a domestic corporation, operates a courier transport business covering a large portion of the United States. X owns and operates a large fleet of automotive vehicles representing a significant volume of independent, homogeneous risks. For valid, non-tax business purposes, X entered into an arrangement with Y, an unrelated domestic corporation, whereby in exchange for an agreed amount of "premiums,"

---

[933] Rev. Rul. 2002-91.
[934] *Harper*, 96 T.C. 45, 58: "whether there was both risk shifting and risk distribution."
[935] Wright, Weber, and Lynch, *Seeking Out Safe Harbors*.

Y "insures" X against the risk of loss arising out of the operation of its fleet in the conduct of its courier business.

The amount of "premiums" under the arrangement is determined at arm's length according to customary insurance industry rating formulas. Y possesses adequate capital to fulfill its obligations to X under the agreement, and in all respects operates in accordance with the applicable requirements of state law. There are no guarantees of any kind in favor of Y with respect to the agreement, nor are any of the "premiums" paid by X to Y in turn loaned back to X. X has no obligation to pay Y additional premiums if X's actual losses during any period of coverage exceed the "premiums" paid by X. X will not be entitled to any refund of "premiums" paid if X's actual losses are lower than the "premiums" paid during any period. In all respects, the parties conduct themselves consistent with the standards applicable to an insurance arrangement between unrelated parties, except that Y does not "insure" any entity other than X.

In this situation, the captive insurance company is completely separate—it has adequate capital, and it operates under its jurisdiction's insurance laws.[936] There are no guarantees offered by the insured relative to the insurance company.[937] "In all respects, the parties conduct themselves consistent with the standards applicable to an insurance arrangement between

---

936  *Id.*
937  *Id.*

unrelated parties, except that Y does not insure any entity other than X."[938] This fact pattern complies with two of the three prongs outlined in *Harper*.[939]

The problem with situation 1 is that there is no risk distribution with the insurance company. That is, because the insurance company only insures one company, the insured's risks are not spread out among other risks. Therefore, there is no insurance.[940]

> Situation 2. The facts are the same as in Situation 1 except that, in addition to its arrangement with X, Y enters into an arrangement with Z, a domestic corporation unrelated to X or Y, whereby in exchange for an agreed amount of "premiums," Y also "insures" Z against the risk of loss arising out of the operation of its own fleet in connection with the conduct of a courier business substantially similar to that of X. The amounts Y earns from its arrangements with Z constitute 10% of Y's total amounts earned during the taxable year on both a gross and net basis. The arrangement with Z accounts for 10% of the total risks borne by Y.

In situation 2, there is insufficient risk distribution because the new insured only accounts for 10 percent of the insurance

---

938  *Id.*
939  *Harper*, 96 T.C. 45, 58: "(1) whether the arrangement involves the existence of an 'insurance risk,' … (3) whether the arrangement was for 'insurance' in its commonly accepted sense."
940  *Harper*, 96 T.C. 45, 58: "whether there was both risk shifting and risk distribution."

company's risk pool.[941] Therefore, this is not insurance for federal income tax purposes.[942]

> Situation 3. X, a domestic corporation, operates a courier transport business covering a large portion of the United States. X conducts the courier transport business through 12 limited liability companies (LLCs) of which it is the single member. The LLCs are disregarded as entities separate from X under the provisions of § 301.7701-3 of the Procedure and Administration Regulations. The LLCs own and operate a large fleet of automotive vehicles, collectively representing a significant volume of independent, homogeneous risks. For valid, non-tax business purposes, the LLCs entered into arrangements with Y, an unrelated domestic corporation, whereby in exchange for an agreed amount of "premiums," Y "insures" the LLCs against the risk of loss arising out of the operation of the fleet in the conduct of their courier business. None of the LLCs account for less than 5%, or more than 15%, of the total risk assumed by Y under the agreements.
>
> The amount of "premiums" under the arrangement is determined at arm's length according to customary insurance industry rating formulas. Y possesses adequate capital to fulfill its obligations to the LLCs under the agreement, and in all respects operates in accordance with the licensing and other requirements

---

941  Id. See also Rev. Rul. 2002-89.
942  Rev. Rul. 2005-40.

of state law. There are no guarantees of any kind in favor of Y with respect to the agreements, nor are any of the "premiums" paid by the LLCs to Y in turn loaned back to X or to the LLCs. No LLC has any obligation to pay Y additional premiums if that LLC's actual losses during the arrangement exceed the "premiums" paid by that LLC. No LLC will be entitled to a refund of "premiums" paid if that LLC's actual losses are lower than the "premiums" paid during any period. Y retains the risks that it assumes under the agreement. In all respects, the parties conduct themselves consistent with the standards applicable to an insurance arrangement between unrelated parties, except that Y does not "insure" any entity other than the LLCs.

In situation 3, the insured "companies" are disregarded for federal income tax purposes, and therefore, the entire group is treated as a sole proprietorship.[943] As a result, the court cannot treat each individual company as a separate legal entity under *Moline Properties*. Therefore, insurance does not exist.[944]

> Situation 4. The facts are the same as in Situation 3, except that each of the 12 LLCs elects pursuant to § 301.7701-3(a) to be classified as an association.[945]

In situation 4, the service will recognize each individual company. Therefore, there is sufficient risk shifting and

---

943  *Id.*
944  *Id.*
945  Rev. Rul. 2005-40.

risk distribution for the IRS to recognize the transaction as insurance for federal tax purposes.[946]

**Revenue Ruling 2002-75**

The primary purpose of this revenue ruling is to state that the service will offer guidance in the form of a private letter ruling on whether there is adequate risk shifting and distribution to qualify for an insurance deduction under 26 U.S.C. 162, and whether there is sufficient risk shifting and distribution to determine if a company is an insurance company for federal income tax purposes.[947] Therefore, once a company has performed all of the initial analysis, it can submit a request to the service for a determination of whether the service will recognize the transaction and the company for tax purposes. While this increases the up-front cost, it does prevent the possibility of a tax problem with the IRS.

**Conclusion**

The following conclusions are based on a summation of all the preceding cases.

The reserve cases are still good law. A company cannot simply foresee a contingency, set aside money for that contingency, and then deduct payments made to the contingency fund. There are two reasons for this. The first is a strict reading of the "ordinary and necessary" business deduction statute, which does not contain any specific statement regarding contributions

---

946 *Id.*
947 Wright, Weber, and Lynch, *Seeking Out Safe Harbors.*

to reserves. Second, allowing this deduction would encourage earnings manipulation. A contemporary example of this concern occurred in 2006 when Exxon earned a record amount of revenue. At the time, there were calls for a windfall profits tax on the company. If Exxon could set aside money in a reserve for this contingency and then deduct the payment to the fund, Exxon could manipulate its earnings. In the year of the deduction, it could lower its taxable income be claiming there was a possible contingency, and then when its taxable income was low, it could argue the contingency no longer existed (and it would not, as there would be no windfall profits) and then bring the reserve back onto its balance sheet.

*Carnation* and *Clougherty* are still good law—that is, a parent cannot be the sole shareholder and insured of the captive and deduct the payment to the captive as an ordinary business expense. However, dicta from several cases lead to the conclusion that other arrangements are possible. The court in *Gulf Oil* noted that "a single insured can have sufficient unrelated risks to achieve adequate risk distribution."[948] This implies that if the captive insures a large number of different risks, such as property/casualty, life, errors and omissions, etc., then risk distribution could occur. Further bolstering this argument is the following statement from *Malone and Hyde*: "Commentators have noted that when an insurer has a sufficiently large number of risks such that great variations in aggregate losses are unlikely, and the premiums received plus its capital make it a viable risk bearer, one can say that risk distribution is present regardless of the number of insureds covered."[949] In addition, it is important

---

948 *Gulf Oil* at 1026.
949 Malone *and Hyde* at 14.

to distinguish this theory from that of Revenue Ruling 2005-40, where the parent only insured one type of risk (automobile). However, this is a legal theory that would most likely be tested in court. To that end, the perfect test case would be a large corporation with a wide range of different risks—workers' compensation, auto, general liability, fire, etc. It would be imperative for the company to have as many different lines of insurance as possible. It would also be incumbent before the formation of the insurer to get several outside opinions from highly accredited sources—preferably PhDs in insurance and risk management—who would sign off on the arrangement, arguing that sufficient risk distribution existed.

Several cases had interlocking directories between the parent and the captive. This indicates that executives can work for the parent and the captive and not run afoul of the law. However, it would be highly advisable for there to be a clear and distinct separation of duties and pay sources when an executive works for a separate company.

The courts' evolving methodology is revealing. In the initial cases—especially *Carnation* and *Clougherty*—the court simply bought the IRS's argument and glossed over the companies' arguments. However, starting with *Humana* and especially beginning with *Harper*, the courts began to take a far more holistic view of the parent-captive relationship. Instead of merely looking at the parent's balance sheet to see if it had the captive's stock, the courts analyzed the captive to see whether or not it was a legitimate insurance company—whether it wrote industry standard contracts, whether it was adequately capitalized and subject to regulation. In essence, if the company was for all practical purposes a legitimate, stand-alone insurance company, the courts were far more likely to accept the arrangement.

Lack of initial capitalization is fatal. This is the reason several companies lost cases. All US jurisdictions with captive insurance statutes have minimum capital levels. Additionally, most jurisdictions allow the insurance commissioner to increase the minimum amount of capital based on the "type, volume and nature" of the insurance underwritten.

When creating a captive, it is imperative to keep the *Harper* factors in mind, in addition to how the courts will apply these factors. To review, *Harper*'s three-prong test is

(1) whether the arrangement involves the existence of an "insurance risk";
(2) whether there was both risk shifting and risk distribution; and
(3) whether the arrangement was for "insurance" in its commonly accepted sense.[950]

Factor 1 requires the petitioner to demonstrate that there is a potential risk as opposed to an investment risk. This is a fairly easy prong to meet. It simply requires the petitioner to demonstrate that the company faces a hazard. The cases reviewed involve risks such as deep-sea ocean drilling, medical malpractice, products liability, marine, and general liability. These are easy to demonstrate, as all companies face (at minimum) general liability.

---

950  *Id.*

Factor two involves the factors from *Helvering*. Risk shifting means that the insured shifts its risk to the insurer. Put another way, when event X happens, the insurance company pays a fixed sum of money to the insured. The best way to demonstrate this is the existence of an insurance policy that conforms to industry norms. Most of the cases involved forms written by an insurance professional who had been in the insurance industry for some time. As such, the forms conformed to traditional notions of insurance as seen from the insurance industry's perspective. Risk distribution is seen from the insurance company's perspective; the insurance company must insure a certain percentage of non-parent risks. Under *Harper*, this amount is 30 percent, but under the IRS's rules, the figure is 50 percent.

A company can establish factor 3 in several ways. In some cases, the company used expert opinion. In others, the court simply looked at the facts of the company to determine whether the captive operated in the same manner as a legitimate insurance company. At minimum, the captives in the cases established reserves, used arm's-length prices in determining insurance rates, were financially capable of paying claims, and issued valid and binding contracts.

Revenue Ruling 2002-89 provides a good synopsis of the above-mentioned elements:

> The amounts P pays to S under the arrangement are established according to customary industry rating formulas. In all respects, the parties conduct themselves consistently with the standards applicable to an insurance arrangement between unrelated parties.

In implementing the arrangement, S may perform all necessary administrative tasks, or it may outsource those tasks at prevailing commercial market rates. P does not provide any guarantee of S's performance, and all funds and business records of P and S are separately maintained. S does not loan any funds to P.

Loans between the captive and the parent are not encouraged. Several revenue rulings' hypothetical fact patterns specifically state that there were no loans between the captive and the parent. However, there is no case law on point in this area. In addition, the conditions outlined in *Harper* specifically state the insurance company must essentially function like a viable insurance company, one of the functions of which is making loans. In addition, it is difficult to fathom the idea that large multi-national companies that currently have captives are not making loans between the captive and the parent or subsidiaries at market rates and under market terms.

In addition, assume the following facts. A captive's operations comply with IRS revenue ruling guidelines. The captive makes a loan to the parent. The loan is made at market rates and complies with lending industry norms in every way. Under what legal theory could the IRS successfully challenge this transaction? While the fact patterns of several revenue rulings have stated that there were no loans between the captive and the parent, there is no legal reason for a court to void a parent-captive loan if the loan is made at market rates and conforms to industry norms.

# Bibliography

Adkisson, Jay. *Captive Insurance Companies*. Bloomington, IN: iUniverse, 2006.

Bankman, Joseph. "The Economic Substance Doctrine." Southern California Law Review 74, no. 5 (2000).

BNA Tax Management. *The Economic Substance Doctrine*. Portfolio 508-1st.

Brown, Michael D. *Structuring and Operating a Captive Self-Insurance Program: Regulatory Aspects*. New York, New York: Practicing Law Institute, 1986.

Hariton, David P. "Sorting Out the Tangle of Economic Substance." *Tax Lawyer* 52, no. 2 (1999): 235-273.

Keinan, Yoram. "It IS Time For the Supreme Court to Voice Its Opinion on Economic Substance." *Houston Business and Tax Law Journal* 7 (2006): 93-137.

Keinan, Yoram. "Rethinking the Role of the Judicial Step Transactions Principle and a Proposal for Codification." *Akron Law Tax Journal* 22 (2007): 45-100.

Moody, Michael J. "Actuarial Involvement in Captive Formations." *Rough Notes*, April 2006, page 158

Moore, Karen Nelson. "The Sham Transaction Doctrine: An Outmoded and Unnecessary Approach to Combating Tax Avoidance." *Florida Law Review* 41 (1989): 659-719.

Pietruszkiewicz, Christopher M. "Economic Substance and the Standard of Review." *Alabama Law Review* 60 (2009): 339-376.

Rosenberg, Joshua. "Tax Avoidance and Income Measurement." *Michigan Law Review* 87 (1998): 365-497.

Taylor, Greg and Scott Sobel. "A Closer Look at Captive Insurance." *CPA Journal*, June 2008, available online at: http://findarticles.com/p/articles/mi_qa5346/is_200806/ai_n27995048/.

Theriault, Patrick. *What to Consider When Establishing and Operating Captives*. Wilmington Trust Company, 2008.

Warner, John P. "Statutory, Regulatory and Common Law Anti-Abuse Weapons." *PLI/Tax* 519 (2001): PLI Course Handbook, Tax Strategies for Corporate Acquisitions, Dispositions, Spin-Offs, Joint Ventures, Financings, Reorganizations & Restructurings 2002.

Westover, Kathryn. *Captives and the Management of Risk*. Dallas, TX: International Risk Management Institute, 2002.

Westover, Kathryn A. *Captive Practices and Procedures*. Dallas, TX: International Risk Management Institute, 2006.

Wright, Bruce, John Weber, and Arthur J. Lynch. *Seeking Out Safe Harbors*. New York, New York LeBoeuf, Lamb, Green and MacRae, 2003.

# Table of Cases

Appeal of Consolidated Asphalt, 1 B.T.A. 79 (1924).

Appeal of William J. Ostheimer, 1 B.T.A. 18 (1924).

Appeal of Pan American Hide, 1 B.T.A. 1249 (1925).

Amerco and Subsidiaries and Republic Western Insurance Company v. C.I.R., 96 T.C. 18 (1991), aff'd Amerco, Inc.; Republic Insurance, 979 F.2d 162 (9th Cir. 1991).

Beech Aircraft v. United States, 1984 WL 988.

Carnation Co. v. Commissioner, 640 F.2d 1010 (9th Cir. 1981).

Carnation Co. v. C.I.R., 71 T.C. 400 (1978), aff'd Carnation Co. v. C.I.R. 640 F.2d 1010 (9th Cir. 1981).

Clougherty Packing Co. v. C.I.R., 84 T.C. 948 (1985), aff'd. Cougherty Packing Co. v. C.I.R., 811 F.2d 1297 (9th Cir. Cal. 1987).

Consumers Oil Corporation of Trenton v. United States, 166 F. Supp. 796 (New Jersey 1960).

Crawford Fitting Co. v. United States, 606 F.Supp. 136 (N.D. Ohio 1985).

Gregory v. Helvering, 293 U.S. 465 (1935).

Goldstein v. C.I.R., 362 F.2d 734 (2nd Cir. 1966).

Gulf Oil v. C.I.R., 914 F.2d 396 (3rd Cir. 1990).

The Harper Group v. C.I.R., 96 T.C. 45, 47 (1991), aff'd The Harper Group v. C.I.R., 979 F.2d 1341 (9th Cir. 1992).

Helvering v. LeGierse, 312 U.S. 531 (1941).

Humana v. Commissioner, 88 T.C. 197, 219, rev'd in part Humana v. Commissioner, 881 F.2d 247 (6th Cir. 1989).

Kidde Industries, Inc. v. United States, 40 Fed. Cl. 42 (1997).

King Enterprises v. United States, 418 F. 2d 511 (Ct. Cl. 1969).

Lucas v. American Code Co., 280 U.S. 445 (1930).

Malone and Hyde, Inc. and Subsidiaries, T.C. Memo. 1989-604 (1989).

Moline Properties v. C.I.R., 319 U.S. 436 (1943).

Mobil Oil Corp. v. United States, 8 Cl. Ct. 555 (1985).

Ocean Drilling and Exploration Company v. United States, 988 F.2d 1135 (Fed. Cir. 1993).

Rev. Rul. 60-275.

Rev. Rul. 64-72.

Rev. Rul. 77-316.

Rev. Rul. 88-72.

Rev. Rul. 2001-31.

Rev. Rul. 2002-45.

Rev. Rul. 2002-89.

Rev. Rul. 2002-90.

Rev. Rul. 2002-91.

Rev. Rul. 2005-40.

Sears Roebuck and Co. v. C.I.R., 96 T.C. 61(1991), aff'd in part, rev'd in part Sears Roebuck and Co. v. C.I.R., 972 F.2d 858 (7th Cir. 1992).

Spring Canyon Coal v. C.I.R., 43 F.2d 78 (10th Cir.1930).

Stearns-Rogers Corp., Inc. v. United States, 577 F. Supp. 833 (Colorado 1984), aff'd Stearns-Rogers Corp., Inc. v. United States, 774 F.2d. 414 (10th Cir. 1985).

United Parcel Service of America, Inc. v. C.I.R., T.C. Memo 1999-268, rev'd United Parcel Service of America v. C.I.R., 254 F.3d 1014, 1016 (11th Cir. 2001).

Weber Paper Company v. United States, 204 F. Supp. 394 (Western District Missouri 1962), aff'd United States v. Weber Paper Company, 320 F.2d 199 (8th Cir. 1963).

# Table of Statutes

Treas. Reg. Section 1.162-1(a)
Treas. Reg. Section 1.801-3(b)
Treas. Reg. Section 1.832-4(a)(3)
Treas. Reg. Section 1.832-4(a)(4)(ii)(A)-(C)
Treas. Reg. Section 1.832-4(a)(5)(i)
Treas. Reg. Section 1.832-4(a)(5)(ii)
Treas. Reg. Section 1.832-4(a)(5)(iii)
Treas. Reg. Section 1.832-4(a)(5)(iv)
Treas. Reg. Section 1.832-4(a)(5)(v)
Treas. Reg. Section 1.832-4(a)(5)(vii)(A)-(B)
Treas. Reg. Section 1.832-4(a)(6)(ii)(A)-(C)
Treas. Reg. Section 1.832-4(a)(8)(i)
Treas. Reg. Section 1.832-4(a)(9)
Treas. Reg. Section 1.832-4(b)
Treas. Reg. Section 1.832-4(c)
Treas. Reg. Section 1.832-4(e)

26 U.S.C. 11(b) (2009)
26 U.S.C. 103(a) (2009)
26 U.S.C. 162(a) (2009)
26 U.S.C. 163 (2009)
28 U.S.C. 164(a) (2009)

26 U.S.C. 501(c)(15)(a)(i)(I) and (II)
26 U.S.C. 816(a) (2009)
26 U.S.C. 831(a) (2009)
26 U.S.C. 831(b)(1) (2009)
26 U.S.C. 831(b)(2)(A)(i)
26 U.S.C. 831(b)(2)(A)(ii) (2009)
26 U.S.C. 832(b)(1)(A) (2009)
26 U.S.C. 832(b)(1)(B) (2009)
26 U.S.C. 832(b)(2) (2009)
26 U.S.C. 832(b)(3) (2009)
26 U.S.C. 832(b)(4)(2009)
26 U.S.C. 832(b)(5)(A) (2009)
26 U.S.C. 832(b)(5)(A)(i)-(iii) (2009)
26 U.S.C. 832(b)(5)(B)(i) (2009)
26 U.S.C. 832(b)(5)(B)(ii)(I) (2009)
26 U.S.C. 832(b)(5)(B)(ii)(II) (2009)
26 U.S.C. 832(b)(5)(B)(iii) (2009)
26 U.S.C. 832(b)(5)(C)(ii)(I)-(I) (2009)
26 U.S.C. 832(b)(6) (2009)
26 U.S.C. 832(c)(1) (2009)
26 U.S.C. 832(c)(2) (2009)
26 U.S.C. 832(c)(3) (2009)
26 U.S.C. 832(c)(4) (2009)
26 U.S.C. 832(c)(5) (2009)
26 U.S.C. 832(c)(6) (2009)
26 U.S.C. 832(c)(7) (2009)
26 U.S.C. 832(c)(8) (2009)
26 U.S.C. 832(c)(9) (2009)
26 U.S.C. 832(c)(10) (2009)
26 U.S.C. 832(c)(11) (2009)
26 U.S.C. 832(c)(12) (2009)

26 U.S.C. 832(d) (2009)
26 U.S.C. 832(e)(3) (2009)
26 U.S.C. 834(a) (2009)
26 U.S.C. 834(b)(1)(A) (2009)
26 U.S.C. 834(b)(1)(B) (2009)
26 U.S.C. 834(b)(1)(C) (2009)
26 U.S.C. 834(b)(1)(D) (2009)
26 U.S.C. 834(b)(2) (2009)
26 U.S.C. 834(c)(1) (2009)
26 U.S.C. 834(c)(3) (2009)
26 U.S.C. 834(c)(4) (2009)
26 U.S.C. 834(c)(5) (2009)
26 U.S.C. 834(c)(6) (2009)
26 U.S.C. 834(c)(7) (2009)
26 U.S.C. 834(c)(8)(A)
26 U.S.C. 834(c)(8)(B)
26 U.S.C. 846(a)(2)(B) (2009)
26 U.S.C. 846(b)(1) (2009)
26 U.S.C. 846(b)(2)(A) (2009)
26 U.S.C. 846(b)(2)(B) (2009)
26 U.S.C. 846(c)(2)(A) (2009)
26 U.S.C. 846(d)(1)
26 U.S.C. 846(e) (2009)
26 U.S.C. 846(e)(2)(B) (2009)
26 U.S.C. 846(e)(2)(C) (2009)
26 U.S.C. 952(a)(1) (2009)
26 U.S.C. 953(a)(1) (2009)
26 U.S.C. 953(c) (2009)
26 U.S.C. 953(c)(1) (2009)
26 U.S.C. 953(d)(1)(A) (2009)
26 U.S.C. 953(d)(1)(B) (2009)

26 U.S.C. 953(d)(2)(A) (2009)
26 U.S.C. 953(e)(2)(A) (2009)
26 U.S.C. 953(e)(2)(B)(i)(I) (2009)
26 U.S.C. 953(e)(2)(B)(i)(II) (2009)
26 U.S.C. 953(e)(3) (2009)
26 U.S.C. 953(e)(3)(A) (2009)
26 U.S.C. 953(e)(3)(B) (2009)
26 U.S.C. 953(e)(3)(C) (2009)
26 U.S.C. 953(e)(6) (2009)
26 U.S.C. 954(d)(3) (2009)
26 U.S.C. 957(a) (2009)
26 U.S.C. 1501 (2009)
26 U.S.C. 1504 (2009)
15 U.S.C. 3901(a)(4) (2009)
15 U.S.C. 3901(a)(4)(A) (2009)
15 U.S.C. 3901(a)(4)(B) (2009)
15 U.S.C. 3901(a)(4)(D) (2009)
15 U.S.C. 3901(a)(4)(E) (2009)
15 U.S.C. 3901(a)(4)(F) (2009)
15 U.S.C. 3901(a)(5) (2009)
15 U.S.C. 3902(1) (2009)

CPSIA information can be obtained at www.ICGtesting.com
Printed in the USA
LVOW12s0824060314

376282LV00001B/23/P